lonely planet

CHÂTEAUX OF THE LOIRE VALLEY

ROAD TRIPS

This edition written and researched by

**Alexis Averbuck, Oliver Berry,
Jean-Bernard Carillet, Gregor Clark**

HOW TO USE THIS BOOK

Reviews

In the Destinations section:

All reviews are ordered in our authors' preference, starting with their most preferred option. Additionally:

Sights are arranged in the geographic order that we suggest you visit them and, within this order, by author preference.

Eating and Sleeping reviews are ordered by price range (budget, midrange, top end) and, within these ranges, by author preference.

Map Legend

Routes

- Trip Route
- Trip Detour
- Linked Trip
- Walk Route
- Tollway
- Freeway
- Primary
- Secondary
- Tertiary
- Lane
- Unsealed Road
- Plaza/Mall
- Steps
-)═(Tunnel
- Pedestrian Overpass
- Walk Track/Path

Boundaries

- ─ ─ ─ International
- ─ ─ ─ State/Province
- Cliff
- Wall

Population

- ❂ Capital (National)
- ◉ Capital (State/Province)
- ● City/Large Town
- ○ Town/Village

Transport

- ✈ Airport
- Cable Car/ Funicular
- ℗ Parking
- Train/Railway
- Tram
- Ⓜ Underground Train Station

Trips

- 1 Trip Numbers
- 9 Trip Stop
- Walking tour
- Trip Detour

Route Markers

- E44 E-road network
- M100 National network

Hydrography

- River/Creek
- Intermittent River
- Swamp/Mangrove
- Canal
- Water
- Dry/Salt/ Intermittent Lake
- Glacier

Areas

- Beach
- Cemetery (Christian)
- Cemetery (Other)
- Park
- Forest
- Urban Area
- Sportsground

Symbols In This Book

- ✔ Top Tips
- 🔗 Link Your Trips
- Tips from Locals
- Trip Detour
- 📖 History & Culture
- 👪 Family
- 🍴 Food & Drink
- 🌳 Outdoors
- 📷 Essential Photo
- 🚶 Walking Tour
- ✗ Eating
- 🛏 Sleeping

- ◉ Sights
- 🏖 Beaches
- 🏃 Activities
- 🎓 Courses
- ☞ Tours
- ✦ Festivals & Events
- 🛏 Sleeping
- ✗ Eating
- 🍷 Drinking
- ☆ Entertainment
- 🛍 Shopping
- ℹ Information & Transport

These symbols and abbreviations give vital information for each listing:

- ☎ Telephone number
- ⏰ Opening hours
- Ⓟ Parking
- ⊘ Nonsmoking
- ❄ Air-conditioning
- @ Internet access
- 📶 Wi-fi access
- ☲ Swimming pool
- 🌱 Vegetarian selection
- 📖 English-language menu
- 👪 Family-friendly

- 🐾 Pet-friendly
- 🚌 Bus
- ⛴ Ferry
- 🚊 Tram
- 🚆 Train
- apt apartments
- d double rooms
- dm dorm beds
- q quad rooms
- r rooms
- s single rooms
- ste suites
- tr triple rooms
- tw twin rooms

CONTENTS

PLAN YOUR TRIP

Welcome to the Loire Valley
& Burgundy 5

Loire Valley
& Burgundy Map 6

Loire Valley
& Burgundy Highlights 8

Paris City Guide 10

Need to Know 14

ROAD TRIPS

1 Châteaux
of the Loire   5 Days   19

2 Caves & Cellars
of the Loire   3 Days   29

3 Medieval
Burgundy   6 Days   39

4 Route des Grands
Crus   2 Days   47

DESTINATIONS

Loire Valley 56
Orléans 57
Blois 61
Château de Chambord 65

Château de Cheverny 66
Château de Chaumont 66
Tours 67
Château de Chenonceau 72
Amboise 72
Château de Villandry 75
Château de Langeais 75
Château d'Azay-le-Rideau 76
Château d'Ussé 77
Chinon 77
Saumur 79
Angers 85
Burgundy 89
Côte d'Or Vineyards 89
Beaune 93
Noyers-sur-Serein 98
Vézelay 99
Autun 101
Cluny 103

ROAD TRIP ESSENTIALS

France Driving
Guide 107

France Travel
Guide 113

Language 121

Vineyards near Beaune, Burgundy's viticultural capital

WELCOME TO
THE LOIRE VALLEY & BURGUNDY

World-renowned châteaux and fine wines may be the two most obvious reasons to visit the Loire Valley and Burgundy, but they're only the tip of the iceberg. This region is home to one of the largest concentrations of cave dwellings and some of Europe's finest medieval architecture. When you've had your fill of château gawking and vineyard hopping, make some time for roads less travelled: go underground to discover the Loire's ancient troglodyte culture; or spend a week exploring Burgundy's medieval churches, abbeys and walled towns.

LOIRE VALLEY & BURGUNDY

★

Châteaux of the Loire
1
Discover a world of caves and wine cellars and savour some of the region's finest food and wine.
5 DAYS

Dreux

A11

Laval

Le Mans

SARTHE

MAYENNE

Ecommoy

A28

Loir

Vendôme

F d'O

Orléa

Mer

Durtal

Blois

Chambord

ANJOU

Baugé

TOURAINE

Angers

Nazelles-Négron

Mûrs-Erigné

Mazé

Parc Naturel Régional Loire Anjou Touraine

Tours

Montlouis-sur-Loire

Doué-la-Fontaine

Saumur

D7

Bléré

A85

Esvres

Vihiers

Chinon

INDRE-ET-LOIRE

Montreuil-Bellay

Vatan

Châtillon-sur-Indre

Levroux

Descartes

Châteauroux

DEUX-SÈVRES

INDRE

Poitiers

La Châ

Caves & Cellars of the Loire
2
France's greatest châteaux, from medieval towers to royal palaces.
3 DAYS

A1C

A20

Niort

Guéret

CREU

N 0   0
100 km
50 miles

Aubus

CHARENTE

HAUTE-VIENNE

Saintes

Limoges

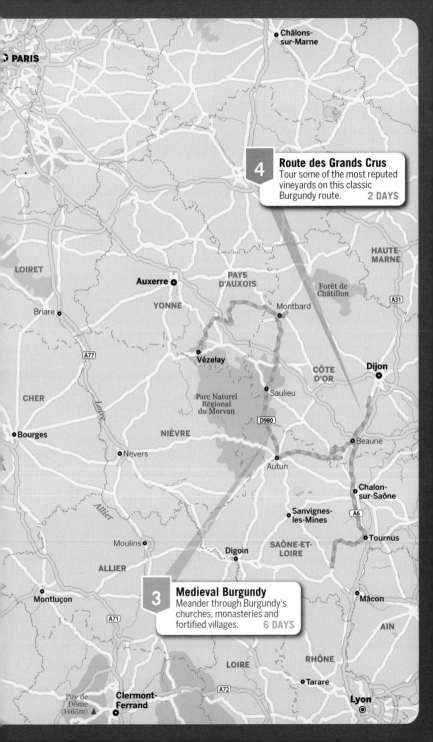

○ PARIS

Châlons-
sur-Marne

4 **Route des Grands Crus**
Tour some of the most reputed
vineyards on this classic
Burgundy route. **2 DAYS**

HAUTE-
MARNE

LOIRET

PAYS
D'AUXOIS

Auxerre ○

YONNE

Forêt de
Châtillon

A31

Briare ○

Montbard

A77

Vézelay

CÔTE
D'OR

Dijon

CHER

Parc Naturel
Régional
du Morvan

Saulieu

D980

Loire

○ Bourges

NIÈVRE

○ Nevers

Beaune

Autun

Chalon-
sur-Saône

Allier

Sanvignes-
les-Mines

A6

○ Tournus

Moulins ○

Digoin

SAÔNE-ET-
LOIRE

ALLIER

3 **Medieval Burgundy**
Meander through Burgundy's
churches, monasteries and
fortified villages. **6 DAYS**

Mâcon

Montluçon

A71

AIN

LOIRE

RHÔNE

A72

Tarare

Puy de
Dôme
(1465m) ▲

Clermont-
Ferrand

Lyon

Château de Chambord
(left) French Renaissance architecture at its finest and fanciest. See it on Trip [1]

Turquant (above right)
Picturesque town nestled into cave-riddled cliffs. Pay a visit on Trip [2]

Puligny-Montrachet (right)
Home to some of Burgundy's most extraordinary white wines. Enjoy on Trip [4]

PARIS

PARIS

If ever a city needed no introduction, it's Paris – a trend setter, fashion former and style icon for centuries, and still very much at the cutting edge. Whether you're here to tick off the landmarks or seek out the secret corners, Paris fulfils all your expectations, and still leaves you wanting more.

Eiffel Tower at dusk

Getting Around

Driving in Paris is a nightmare. Happily, there's no need for a car. The metro is fast, frequent and efficient; tickets cost €1.70 (day passes €6.70) and are valid on the city's buses. Bikes can be hired from 1800 Vélib (www.velib.paris.fr) stations; insert a credit card, authorise a €150 deposit and pedal away. Day passes cost €1; first 30 minutes free, subsequent 30 minutes from €2.

Parking

Meters don't take coins; use a chip-enabled credit card. Municipal car parks cost €2 to €3.50 an hour, or €20 to €25 per 24 hours.

Discover the Taste of Paris

Le Marais is one of the best areas for eating out, with its small restaurants and trendy bistros. Don't miss Paris' street markets: the Marché Bastille, rue Montorgueil and rue Mouffetard are full of atmosphere.

Live Like a Local

Base yourself in Montmartre for its Parisian charm, if you don't mind crowds. Le Marais and Bastille provide style on a budget, while St-Germain is good for a splurge.

Useful Websites

Paris Info (http://en.parisinfo.com) Official visitor site.

Lonely Planet (www.lonelyplanet.com/paris) Lonely Planet's city guide.

Secrets of Paris (www.secretsofparis.com) Local's blog full of insider tips.

Paris by Mouth (www.parisbymouth.com) Eat and drink your way round the capital.

For more, check out our city and country guides. www.lonelyplanet.com

TOP EXPERIENCES

➡ Eiffel Tower at Twilight

Any time is a good time to take in the panorama from the top of the 'Metal Asparagus' (as Parisians snidely call it) – but the twilight view is extra special (www.toureiffel.fr).

➡ Musée du Louvre

France's greatest repository of art, sculpture and artefacts, the Louvre is a must-visit – but don't expect to see it all in a day (www.louvre.fr).

➡ Basilique du Sacré-Coeur

Climb inside the cupola of this Montmartre landmark for one of the best cross-city vistas (www.sacre -coeur-montmartre.com).

➡ Musée d'Orsay

Paris' second-most-essential museum, with a fabulous collection encompassing originals by Cézanne, Degas, Monet, Van Gogh and more (www.musee-orsay.fr).

➡ Cathédrale de Notre-Dame

Peer over Paris from the north tower of this Gothic landmark, surrounded by gargoyles and flying buttresses (www.cathedraledeparis.com).

➡ Les Catacombes

Explore more than 2km of tunnels beneath the streets of Montparnasse, lined with the bones and skulls of millions of Parisians (www. catacombes.paris.fr).

➡ Cimetière Père-Lachaise

Oscar Wilde, Edith Piaf, Marcel Proust and Jim Morrison are just a few of the famous names buried in this wildly overgrown cemetery (www. perelachaise.com).

➡ Canal St-Martin

Join the locals for a walk or bike ride along the tow-paths of this 4.5km canal, once derelict but now reborn as a haven from the city hustle.

STRETCH YOUR LEGS
PARIS

Start Place de la Concorde

Finish Place du Panthéon

Distance 4.5km

Duration Three hours

Paris is one of the world's most strollable cities, whether that means window-shopping on the boulevards or getting lost among the lanes of Montmartre. This walk starts by the Seine, crosses to the Île de la Cité and finishes in the Latin Quarter, with monuments and museums aplenty en route.

Place de la Concorde

If it's Parisian vistas you're after, the place de la Concorde makes a fine start. From here you can see the Arc de Triomphe, the Assemblée Nationale (the lower house of parliament), the Jardin des Tuileries and the Seine. Laid out in 1755, the square was where many aristocrats lost their heads during the Revolution, including Louis XVI and Marie Antoinette. The obelisk in the centre originally stood in the Temple of Ramses at Thebes (now Luxor).

The Walk >> Walk east through the Jardin des Tuileries.

Jardin des Tuileries

This 28-hectare landscaped **garden** (🕙7am-7.30pm, 9pm or 11pm) was laid out in 1664 by André Le Nôtre, who also created Versailles' gardens. Filled with fountains, ponds and sculptures, the gardens are now part of the Banks of the Seine World Heritage Site, created by Unesco in 1991.

The Walk >> Walk across place du Carrousel onto the Cour Napoleon.

Musée du Louvre

Overlooking the Cour Napoleon is the mighty Louvre, with its controversial 21m-high glass **Grande Pyramide**, designed by IM Pei in 1989. Nearby is the **Pyramide Inversée** (Upside-Down Pyramid), which acts as a skylight for the underground Carrousel du Louvre shopping centre.

The Walk >> Continue southeast along the riverside Quai du Louvre to the Pont Neuf metro station.

Pont Neuf

As you cross the Seine, you'll walk over Paris' oldest bridge – ironically known as the 'New Bridge', or Pont Neuf. Henri IV inaugurated the bridge in 1607 by crossing it on a white stallion.

The Walk >> Cross the Pont Neuf onto the Île de la Cité. Walk southeast along Quai des Horloges, and then turn right onto bd du Palais.

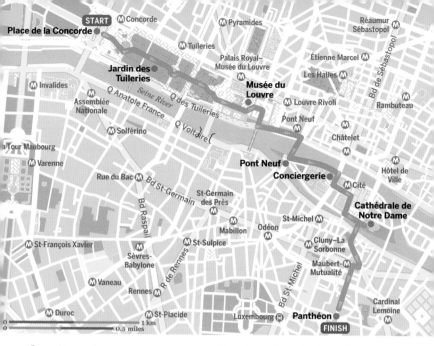

Conciergerie

On bd du Palais, the elegant **Conciergerie** (www.monuments-nationaux.fr; 2 bd du Palais, Île de la Cité, 1e; adult/child €8.50/free; ⏱9.30am-6pm; Ⓜ Cité) is a royal palace that became a prison and torture chamber for enemies of the Revolution. The 14th-century Salle des Gens d'Armes (Cavalrymen's Hall) is Europe's largest surviving medieval hall.

The nearby church of **Sainte-Chapelle** (combined ticket with Conciergerie €12.50/free) has stunning stained glass.

The Walk » Continue east along rue de Lutèce, then cross place du Parvis Notre Dame and walk towards the cathedral.

Cathédrale de Notre Dame

At the eastern end of Île de la Cité, show-stopper **Notre Dame** (www.cathedraledeparis.com; 6 place du Parvis Notre Dame, 4e; admission free; ⏱7.45am-7pm) is the heart of Paris in more ways than one – it's from here that all distances in France are measured.

Built in stages between the 11th and 15th centuries, it's on a gargantuan scale; the interior alone is 130m long,

48m wide and 35m high. Don't miss the three rose windows, the 7800-pipe organ and a walk up the gargoyle-covered Gothic towers.

The Walk » Cross the river on Pont au Double and follow rue Lagrange to bd St-Germain. Then take rue des Carmes and rue Valette south to the place du Panthéon.

Panthéon

Once you reach the left bank you'll be in the Latin Quarter, the centre of Parisian higher education since the Middle Ages, and still home to the city's top university, the Sorbonne.

It's also where you'll find the **Panthéon** (www.monum.fr; place du Panthéon; adult/child €8.50/free; ⏱10am-6.30pm Apr-Sep, to 6pm Oct-Mar), the neoclassical mausoleum where some of France's greatest thinkers are entombed, including Voltaire, Rousseau and Marie Curie.

The Walk » It's a long walk back, so it's easier to catch the metro. Walk east to place Monge, take Line 7 to Palais Royal Musée du Louvre, then Line 1 west to Concorde.

NEED TO KNOW

CURRENCY
Euro (€)

LANGUAGE
French

VISAS
Generally not required for stays of up to 90 days (or at all for EU nationals); some nationalities need a Schengen visa.

FUEL
Petrol stations are common around main roads and larger towns. Unleaded costs from around €1.60 per litre; *gazole* (diesel) is usually at least €0.15 cheaper.

RENTAL CARS
ADA (www.ada.fr)

Auto Europe (www.autoeurope.com)

Avis (www.avis.com)

Europcar (www.europcar.com)

Hertz (www.hertz.com)

IMPORTANT NUMBERS
Ambulance (📞15)

Police (📞17)

Fire brigade (📞18)

Europe-wide emergency (📞112)

Climate

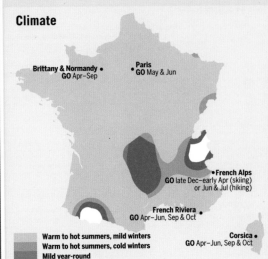

Brittany & Normandy ●
GO Apr–Sep

Paris
● **GO** May & Jun

● **French Alps**
GO late Dec–early Apr (skiing) or Jun & Jul (hiking)

French Riviera ●
GO Apr–Jun, Sep & Oct

Corsica ●
GO Apr–Jun, Sep & Oct

Warm to hot summers, mild winters
Warm to hot summers, cold winters
Mild year-round
Mild summers, cold winters
Alpine climate

When to Go

High Season (Jul & Aug)
» The main holiday season in France – expect traffic jams and big queues, especially in August.

» Christmas, New Year and Easter are also busy times to travel.

» Late December to March is high season in French ski resorts.

Shoulder Season (Apr–Jun & Sep)
» Balmy temperatures, settled weather and light crowds make this an ideal time to travel.

» Hotel rates drop in busy areas such as southern France and the Atlantic coast.

» The *vendange* (grape harvest) happens in early autumn.

Low Season (Oct–Mar)
» Expect heavy discounts on accommodation (sometimes as much as 50%).

» Snow covers the Alps and Pyrenees, as well as much of central France.

» Many sights and hotels close down for winter.

Daily Costs

Budget: Less than €100

» Double room in a budget hotel: €50–70

» Set lunchtime menus: €10–15

Midrange: €100–€200

» Double room in a midrange hotel: €70–120

» À la carte mains: €15–20

Top End: Over €200

» Luxury hotel room: €150–200

» Top-end restaurant meal: menus from €50, à la carte from €80

Eating

Cafes Coffee, drinks and bar snacks.

Bistros Serve anything from light meals to sit-down dinners.

Restaurants Range from simple *auberges* (country inns) to Michelin-starred wonders.

Vegetarians Limited choice on most menus; look out for *restaurants bios* in cities.

In this book, price symbols indicate the cost of a two-course set menu:

€	under €20
€€	€20–40
€€€	more than €40

Sleeping

Hotels France has a wide range of hotels, from budget to luxury. Unless indicated otherwise, breakfast is extra.

Chambres d'hôte The French equivalent of a B&B; prices nearly always include breakfast.

Hostels Most large towns have a hostel operated by the FUAJ (Fédération Unie des Auberges de Jeunesse).

Price symbols indicate the cost of a double room with private bathroom in high season unless otherwise noted:

€	under €80
€€	€80–180
€€€	more than €180

Arriving in France

Aéroport Roissy Charles de Gaulle (Paris)

Rental cars Major car-rental agencies have concessions at arrival terminals.

Trains, buses and RER To Paris centre every 15 to 30 minutes, 5am to 11pm.

Taxis €50 to €60; 30 minutes to Paris centre.

Aéroport d'Orly (Paris)

Rental cars Desks beside the arrivals area.

Orlyval rail, RER and buses At least every 15 minutes, 5am to 11pm.

Taxis €45 to €60; 25 minutes to Paris centre.

Mobile Phones

Most European and Australian phones work, but turn off roaming to avoid heavy data charges. Buying a French SIM card provides much cheaper call rates.

Internet Access

Wi-fi is available in most hotels and B&Bs (usually free, but sometimes for a small charge). Many cafes and restaurants also offer free wi-fi to customers.

Money

ATMs are available everywhere. Most major credit cards are accepted (with the exception of American Express). Larger cities have *bureaux de change*.

Tipping

By law, restaurant and bar prices include *service compris* (a 15% service charge). Taxis expect around 10%; round up bar bills to the nearest euro.

Useful Websites

France Guide (www.franceguide.com) Official website run by the French tourist office.

Lonely Planet (www.lonelyplanet.com/france) Travel tips, accommodation, forum and more.

Mappy (www.mappy.fr) Online tools for mapping and journey planning.

France Meteo (www.meteo.fr) The lowdown on the French weather.

About France (www.about-france.com/travel.htm) Tips for driving in France.

For more, see Road Trip Essentials (p106).

Road Trips

1 **Châteaux of the Loire 5 Days**
Tour France's greatest châteaux, from austere medieval towers to exuberant royal palaces. (p19)

2 **Caves & Cellars of the Loire 3 Days**
Discover the Loire's subterranean world: wine cellars, cave dwellings and mushroom farms. (p29)

3 **Medieval Burgundy 6 Days**
Search for medieval treasures in Burgundy's churches, monasteries and fortified villages. (p40)

4 **Route des Grands Crus 2 Days**
Sample France's most venerable vintages on this wine lover's tour of Burgundy. (p47)

View of Amboise from the Château Royal d'Amboise (p23)
PHOTOGRAPHY BY BOBI/GETTY IMAGES ©

Châteaux of the Loire

1

For centuries, France's great river has been the backdrop for royal intrigue and extravagant architecture. This trip weaves together nine of the Loire Valley's most classic châteaux.

L231, 475

TRIP HIGHLIGHTS

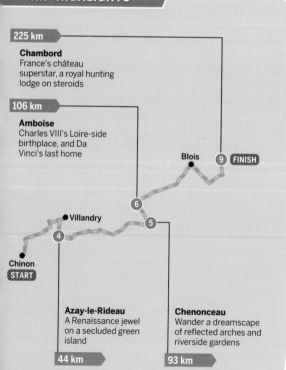

225 km

Chambord
France's château superstar, a royal hunting lodge on steroids

106 km

Amboise
Charles VIII's Loire-side birthplace, and Da Vinci's last home

Blois ● 9 FINISH

6

● Villandry
4
5

Chinon ●
START

Azay-le-Rideau
A Renaissance jewel on a secluded green island

44 km

Chenonceau
Wander a dreamscape of reflected arches and riverside gardens

93 km

5 DAYS
225KM / 140 MILES

GREAT FOR...

BEST TIME TO GO
May and June for good cycling weather; July for gardens and special events.

 ESSENTIAL PHOTO
Chenonceau's graceful arches reflected in the Cher River.

 BEST TWO DAYS
The stretch between Chenonceau and Chambord takes in all the classics.

teau de Villandry (22)

19

1 Châteaux of the Loire

From warring medieval counts to the kings and queens of France, countless powerful figures have left their mark on the Loire Valley. The result is France's most diverse and magnificent collection of castle architecture. This itinerary visits nine of the Loire's most iconic châteaux, running the gamut from austere medieval fortresses to ostentatious royal palaces; midway through, a side trip leads off the beaten track to four lesser-known châteaux.

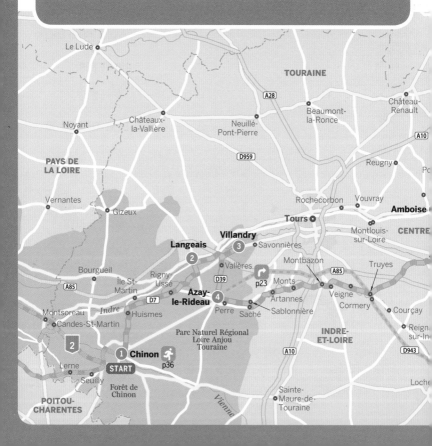

1 Chinon (p77)

Tucked between its medieval fortress and the Vienne River, Chinon is a lovely place to start exploring the magnificent châteaux of central France. The town is forever etched in France's collective memory as the place where Joan of Arc first met future King Charles VII in 1429. Take in all the highlights on our walk (p28), and stay overnight to appreciate the town's relaxed pace.

The Drive » Follow the D16 north of Chinon for 10km, then head 15km east on the D7 past the fairy-tale Château d'Ussé (the inspiration for *Sleeping Beauty*) to Lignières, where you catch the D57 3km north into Langeais.

- - - - - - - - - - - - - -

2 Langeais (p75)

Built in the 1460s to cut off the likely invasion route from Brittany, **Château de Langeais** (www.chateau-de-langeais. com; adult/child €8.50/5; ⏰9.30am-6.30pm Apr– mid-Nov, 10am-5pm mid-Nov–Mar) was designed first and foremost as a fortress. Ironically, three decades later this was the very same château where Charles VIII married Anne of Brittany, bringing about the historic union of France and Brittany and effectively ending the threat of Breton invasion.

One of the few châteaux with its original medieval interior, the castle (reached via a creaky drawbridge) is fantastically preserved inside and out, its flag-stoned rooms filled with 15th-century furniture, its crenellated ramparts and defensive towers jutting out from the jumbled rooftops of the surrounding village.

Up top, stroll the castle's **ramparts** for a soldier's-eye view of the town: gaps underfoot enabled boiling oil, rocks and ordure to be dumped on attackers. Across the courtyard, Langeais' ruined **keep**,

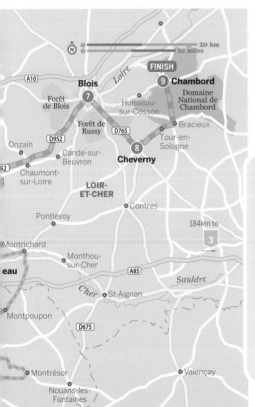

LINK YOUR TRIP

2 Caves & Cellars of the Loire

Tour wineries and centuries-old cave dwellings between Chinon and Saumur.

3 Medieval Burgundy

Three hours east of Blois, steep yourself in the world of Burgundy's medieval churches and abbeys.

constructed in 992 by the granddaddy of medieval power mavens, Foulques Nerra, is the oldest such structure in France.

The Drive ▶ Backtrack south across the Loire on the D57, then follow the riverbank east 10km on the D16 to Villandry.

- - - - - - - - - - -

❸ Villandry (p75)

Renowned for its glorious landscaped gardens, **Château de Villandry** (www.chateauvillandry.com; château & gardens adult/child €9.50/5.50, gardens only €6.50/4.50; ☉9am-6pm Apr-Oct, earlier closing rest of the year, closed mid-Nov–Dec) was the brainchild of Jean le Breton, François I's finance minister and Italian ambassador. Today visitors can stroll pebbled walkways through 6 hectares of formal **water gardens**, a **maze**, **vineyards** and multiple themed gardens including the fabulous 16th-century **potager** (kitchen garden), where even the vegetables are laid out in regimental colour-coordinated fashion. The gardens bloom between April and October, although they're most spectacular in midsummer.

For bird's-eye views across the gardens and the nearby Loire and Cher Rivers, climb to the top of the **donjon** (keep), the only medieval remnant in this otherwise Renaissance-style château.

The Drive ▶ Go southwest 4km on the D7, then turn south 7km on the D39 into Azay-le-Rideau.

- - - - - - - - - -

TRIP HIGHLIGHT

❹ Azay-le-Rideau (p76)

Romantic, moat-ringed **Azay-le-Rideau** (azay-le-rideau.monuments-nationaux.fr/en; adult/child €8.50/free; ☉9.30am-6pm Apr-Sep, to 7pm Jul & Aug, 10am-5.15pm Oct-Mar) is one of France's absolute gems, wonderfully adorned with slender turrets, geometric windows and decorative stonework, all wrapped up within a shady landscaped park on a natural island in middle of the Indre River. Built in the 1500s, the château's most famous feature is its open **loggia staircase**, in the Italian style, overlooking the central courtyard and decorated with the royal salamanders and ermines of François I and Queen Claude. In summer, one of the region's oldest and best **son et lumière** (sound and light) shows is projected onto the castle walls nightly.

The Drive ▶ Follow the D84 east 6km through the tranquil Indre valley, then cross the river south into Saché, home to an attractive château and Balzac museum. From Saché continue 26km east on the D17, 11km northeast on the D45 and 9km east on the D976. Cross north over the Cher River and follow the D40 east 1.5km into Chenonceau.

- - - - - - - - - -

TRIP HIGHLIGHT

❺ Chenonceau (p72)

Spanning the languid Cher River via a series of supremely graceful arches, **Château de Chenonceau** (www.chenonceau.com; adult/child €11/8.50; ☉from 9am or 9.30am year-round, closes 5pm to 8pm depending on month) is a study in elegance, with its remarkable architecture, exquisite landscaping and fabulous furnishings.

Several noteworthy women have left their mark on Chenonceau, hence its alternative name, Le Château des Dames (Ladies' Château). The distinctive arches were added by Diane de Poitiers, mistress of King Henri II. Henri's widow, Catherine de Médici, added the yew-tree **labyrinth** and the western rose garden. In the 18th century, the aristocrat Madame Dupin made Chenonceau a centre of fashionable society and attracted guests including Voltaire and Rousseau. Legend has it that she also single-handedly saved the château from destruction during the Revolution, thanks to her popularity with local villagers.

The château's *pièce de résistance* is the 60m-long window-lined **Grande Gallerie**

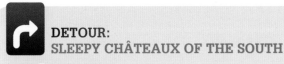

DETOUR:
SLEEPY CHÂTEAUX OF THE SOUTH

Start ➍ Azay-le-Rideau

Escape the crowds by detouring to four less-visited châteaux between Azay-le-Rideau and Chenonceau.

First stop: **Loches**, where Joan of Arc, fresh from her victory at Orléans in 1429, famously persuaded Charles VII to march to Reims and claim the French crown. The undisputed highlight here is the **Cité Royale** (www.chateau-loches.fr; adult/child €7.50/5.50; ⊙9am-7pm Apr-Sep, 9.30am-5pm Oct-Mar), a royal citadel that spans 500 years of French château architecture in a single site, from Foulques Nerra's austere 10th-century **keep** to the Flamboyant Gothic and Renaissance styles of the **Logis Royal**. To get here from Azay-le-Rideau, head 55km east along the D751, A85 and D943.

Next comes the quirky **Château de Montrésor** (www.chateaudemontresor.fr; adult/child €8/4; ⊙10am-7pm Apr-Oct, to 6pm Sat & Sun Nov-Mar), 19km east of Loches on the D760, still furnished much as it was over a century ago when it belonged to Polish count, financier and railroad magnate Xavier Branicki. The eclectic decor includes a Cuban mahogany spiral staircase, a piano once played by Chopin and a treasury room filled with Turkish hookahs and other spoils from the 17th-century Battle of Vienna.

Next, head 20km north on the D10 and D764 to **Château de Montpoupon** (www.chateau-loire-montpoupon.com; adult/child €8/4.50; ⊙10am-7pm), idyllically situated in rolling countryside. Opposite the castle, grab lunch at the wonderful **Auberge de Montpoupon** (www.aubergedemontpoupon.com; menus €21-67; ⊙lunch & dinner daily).

Continue 12km north on the D764 to **Château de Montrichard**, another ruined 11th-century fortress constructed by Foulques Nerra. After visiting the château, picnic in the park by the Cher River, or go wine tasting at **Caves Monmousseau** (www.monmousseau.com; 71 rte de Vierzon; tours adult/child €3.50/free; ⊙10am-noon & 2.30-5.30pm; p74).

From Montrichard, head 10km west on the D176 and D40 to rejoin the main route at Chenonceau.

---

spanning the Cher, scene of many a wild party over the centuries. The gallery was legendarily also used as an escape route for refugees fleeing the Nazi occupation during WWII, when the Cher marked the boundary between free and occupied France.

In summer, don't miss the chance to stroll Chenonceau's illuminated grounds at night during the **Promenade Nocturne** (adult/child €5/free).

The Drive ❯❯ Follow the D81 north 13km into Amboise; 2km south of town, you'll pass the Mini-Châteaux theme park, whose intricate scale models of 44 Loire Valley châteaux are great fun for kids.

TRIP HIGHLIGHT

➏ Amboise (p72)

Elegant Amboise perches on the Loire's southern bank, overlooked by the fortified 15th-century **Château Royal d'Amboise** (www.chateau-amboise.com; adult/child €10/7;

⊙9am-7pm Jul & Aug, to 6pm Apr-Oct, shorter hours Nov-Mar). Thanks to the château's easily defensible position, it saw little military action, serving more often as a weekend getaway from the official royal seat at nearby Blois. Charles VIII, born and bred here, was responsible for the château's Italianate remodelling in 1492.

Just up the street, Amboise's other main sight is **Le Clos Lucé** (www.vinci-closluce.com; adult/

LOCAL KNOWLEDGE
ELSA SAUVÉ,
CHÂTEAU DE
CHAMBORD

The double-helix staircase that whisks visitors from Chambord's ground floor to its rooftop keep is the highlight, the magic being that two people can see each other go up and down it without their paths ever crossing. A magnificent view of the estate unfolds from the rooftop terrace, an unforgettable place with its sculpted chimney and turrets, really a place of contemplation and daydream.

Top: Château de Chambord
Left: Leonardo da Vinci-designed double-helix staircase
Right: Rowing alongside the castle

child €14/8.50; ⊙9am-8pm
Jul & Aug, 9am-7pm Feb-Jun &
Sep-Oct, 9am-6pm Nov-Dec,
10am-6pm Jan), **the grand
manor house where
Leonardo da Vinci took
up residence in 1516 and
spent the final years of
his life at the invitation
of François I. Already 64
by the time he arrived,
da Vinci spent his time
sketching, tinkering
and dreaming up new
contraptions, scale
models of which are now
abundantly displayed
throughout the home and
its expansive gardens.**

The Drive » Follow the D952
northeast along the Loire's
northern bank, enjoying 35km
of beautiful river views en route
to Blois. The town of Chaumont-
sur-Loire makes a pleasant stop
for lunch (see p66) or for its
imposing château and gardens.

❼ Blois (p61)

Straddling a rocky
escarpment on the Loire's
northern bank, the
Château Royal de Blois
(www.chateaudeblois.fr; place
du Château; adult/child €10/5;
⊙9am-6pm Apr-Jun, Oct &
Nov, to 7pm Jul & Aug, shorter
hours rest of year) **bears the
creative mark of several
successive French kings.
More a showpiece than
a military stronghold, its
four grand wings offer a
superb overview of Loire
Valley architectural styles,
with elements of Gothic
(13th century), Flamboyant
Gothic (1498–1503), early
Renaissance (1515–24) and
classical (1630s).**

Highlights include the **loggia staircase**, decorated with salamanders and curly 'F's (François I's heraldic symbols); the **studiolo**, within whose elaborately panelled walls Catherine de Médici allegedly maintained secret cupboards for stashing poisons; and the 2nd-floor **king's apartments**, which witnessed one of the bloodiest episodes in French royal history. In 1588 Henri III had his arch-rival, Duke Henri I de Guise, murdered here by royal bodyguards (the king himself hid behind a tapestry). Period paintings chronicle the gruesome events.

The Drive » Cross the Loire and continue 16km southeast into Cheverny via the D765 and D102.

- - - - - - - - - -

⑧ Cheverny (p66)

A masterpiece of French classical architecture, beautifully proportioned **Château de Cheverny** (www.chateau-cheverny.fr; adult/child €10/7; ☺9am-7pm Apr-Sep, 10am-5pm Oct-Mar) was built between 1625 and 1634 by Jacques Hurault, an *intendant* (royal administrative official) to Louis XII, and has been continuously

inhabited by the same family for four centuries. Highlights of the sumptuously furnished interior include a **formal dining room** decorated with scenes from *Don Quixote* and a **children's playroom** filled with Napoléon III–era toys.

Outside amid sprawling lawns, Cheverny's **kennels** house pedigreed hunting dogs; feeding time, known as the **Soupe des Chiens**, takes place daily at 5pm. Behind the château, the 18th-century **Orangerie**, which sheltered priceless artworks including the *Mona Lisa* during WWII, is now a tearoom.

Tintin fans may recognise the château's façade as the model for Captain Haddock's ancestral home, Marlinspike Hall.

The Drive » Take the D102 10km northeast into Bracieux, then turn north on the D112 for the final 8km run through the forested Domaine National de Chambord (Europe's largest hunting reserve). Catch your first dramatic glimpse of France's most famous château on the right as you arrive in Chambord.

- - - - - - - - - -

TRIP HIGHLIGHT

⑨ Chambord (p65)

For over-the-top splendour, nothing compares to **Château de Chambord** (www.chambord. org; adult/child €11/9, parking €4; ☺9am-6pm Apr-Sep, 10am-5pm Oct-Mar), one of the supreme examples of French Renaissance architecture.

Begun in 1519 as a weekend hunting lodge by François I, it quickly snowballed into France's most ambitious (and expensive) royal architectural project. When construction finally ended 30-odd years later, the castle boasted some 440 rooms, 365 fireplaces and 84 staircases, all built around a rectangular **keep**, crossed by four great hallways and flanked at the corners by circular bastions. Up through the centre of it all winds Chambord's crowning glory, the famous **double-helix staircase** designed by Leonardo da Vinci, with two intertwining flights of stairs leading up to the great **lantern tower** and rooftop, from where you can survey the landscaped grounds and marvel at the exuberant jumble of cupolas, turrets, chimneys and lightning rods.

Château Royal d'Amboise (p23)

Caves & Cellars of the Loire

2

This tour of caves, wine cellars and châteaux explores the best of the western Loire Valley, home to habitations troglodytiques *(cave dwellings) and some of France's finest food and wine.*

TRIP HIGHLIGHTS

39 km

Chinon
Stroll medieval streets in Joan of Arc's footsteps

0 km

Saumur
Home to triple sec, fine dining and France's most acrobatic horses

Brissac

FINISH
St-Hilaire-St-Florent

START

10

Doue-la-Fontaine

Brézé

Fontevraud-l'Abbaye

6

Rochemenier
Explore 1930s cave-dwelling traditions

98 km

Turquant
Cave-riddled cliffs converted to restaurants and galleries

9 km

3 DAYS
160KM / 100 MILES

GREAT FOR...

BEST TIME TO GO

May for greenery; September and October for harvest.

ESSENTIAL PHOTO

Turquant's cliff face, with converted cave dwellings and windmill.

BEST FOR WINE-TASTING

The 15km stretch between St-Hilaire-St-Florent and Montsoreau.

erground chapel, Rochemenier (p34)

2 Caves & Cellars of the Loire

The Loire Valley's soft, easily excavated *tuffeau* (limestone) has been interwoven with local culture for millennia. From Merovingian quarries that did a booming international trade in early Christian sarcophagi, to medieval and Renaissance châteaux, to modern restaurants, mushroom farms and wine cellars adapted from cave dwellings, this tour offers an introduction to local troglodyte culture as well as ample opportunities to savour the region's renowned gastronomy and wines.

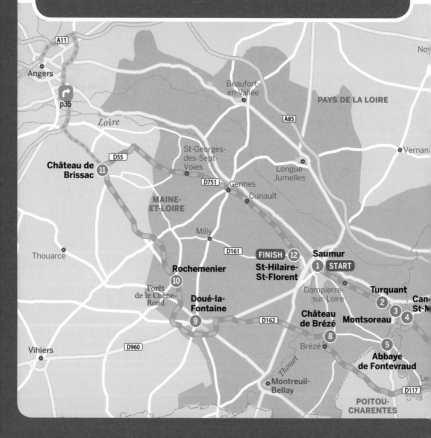

TRIP HIGHLIGHT

① Saumur (p79)

Start your tour in sophisticated Saumur, one of the Loire Valley's great gastronomic and viticultural centres.

For an overview of the region's wine producers, along with free tastings, head to the riverside **Maison du Vin** (7 quai Carnot; ⏱10.30am-12.30pm & 3-6pm Tue-Sat). Next, explore Saumur's other claim to fermented fame at **Distillerie Combier**

(www.combier.fr; 48 rue Beaurepaire; adult €4; ⏱3-5 guided visits per day, 10am-12.30pm & 2-7pm Tue-Sun), where triple sec liqueur was invented in 1834; tours of the still-functioning distillery offer an evocative, behind-the-scenes look at gleaming century-old copper stills, vintage Eiffel machinery and fragrant vats full of Haitian bitter oranges. Around town, make sure to try Saumur's iconic aperitif, *soupe saumuroise* – made with triple sec, lemon juice and sparkling wine.

Other Saumur highlights include the fairy-tale 13th-century **Château de Saumur** (www.chateau-saumur.com; adult/child €9/5; ⏱10am-12.30pm & 2-5.30pm Tue-Sun Apr-Oct, 10am-6.30pm mid-Jun–mid-Sep) and the **École Nationale d'Équitation** (www.cadrenoir.fr; rte de Marson; guided visits adult/child €8/6; ⏱mornings Tue-Sat, afternoons Mon-Fri mid-Apr–mid-Oct), a renowned equestrian academy that's long been responsible for training France's elite Cadre Noir cavalry division and Olympic riding teams. Take a one-hour guided visit (four to 10 daily), or book ahead for one of the not-to-be-missed **Cadre Noir presentations** (adult/child €16/9), semi-monthly 'horse ballets' that show off the horses' astonishing discipline and acrobatic manoeuvres.

The Drive » East of Saumur, the D947 meanders 10km through the towns of Souzay-Champigny and Parnay, home to several tasting rooms, including Château Villeneuve, Clos des Cordeliers, Château de Parnay and Château de Targé. Troglodyte dwellings pockmark the cliff face to your right as a hilltop windmill signals your arrival in Turquant.

TRIP HIGHLIGHT

② Turquant (p82)

Backed by chalk-coloured, cave-riddled cliffs, picturesque Turquant is a showcase for the creative adaptation of historic troglodyte dwellings. The town's 'main street' runs parallel to the D947, past a handful of art galleries, restaurants and other enterprises featuring designer windows and colourful doors wedged into the cliff face. Turn right off the main road to **Le Troglo des Pommes Tapées**

LINK YOUR TRIP

1 Châteaux of the Loire

In Chinon, connect to this classic tour of the Loire Valley's most famous châteaux.

31

(letroglodespommestapees.fr; 11 rue des Ducs d'Anjou; adult/child €6/3.50; ☺2-6.30pm Tue, 10am-12.30pm & 2-6.30pm Wed-Sun mid-Feb–mid-Nov), a giant cave house whose owners have revived the ancient art of oven-drying and painstakingly hammering apples into the local delicacy known as *pommes tapées.* Guided cave tours are followed by tastings of dried apples simmered in red wine. Turquant's *tuffeau* (limestone) cliffs have also been adapted for use as wine cellars by producers such as **La Grande Vignolle** (www.filliatreau.com) and **Domaine des Amandiers** (www.domaine-des-amandiers.com).

The Drive » It's just a 3km hop, skip and jump to Montsoreau along the D947 and D751. Alternatively, follow the narrow Route des Vins (parallel and slightly south of the D947) to the 16th-century windmill Moulin de la Herpinière, then continue into Montsoreau via tiny Chemin de la Herpinière.

- - - - - - - - - - - -

③ Montsoreau (p83)

Looming impressively above the Loire, **Château de Montsoreau** (www.chateau-montsoreau.com; adult/child €9/6; ☺10am-7pm May-Sep, 2-6pm Apr, Oct–mid-Nov & weekends Mar, closed mid-Nov–Feb) was built in 1455 by one of Charles VII's advisers, and later immortalised in Alexandre Dumas' novel, *La Dame de Monsoreau.* The crowning attraction

here is the dazzling view from the rooftop, extending from the Loire's confluence with the Vienne to the domes and turrets of Saumur. On weekends, enjoy free wine tasting in the castle's cellars.

Nearby, the **Maison du Parc** (www.parc-loire-anjou-touraine.fr; 15 av de la Loire; ☺9.30am-7pm) offers information on the Parc Naturel Régional Loire-Anjou-Touraine, which protects 2530 sq km of the surrounding landscape.

The Drive » Follow the D751 1km southeast into Candes-St-Martin, enjoying pretty river views on your left.

- - - - - - - - - - - -

④ Candes-St-Martin (p83)

Recognised as one of France's prettiest villages, Candes-St-Martin occupies an idyllic spot at the confluence of the Vienne and the Loire Rivers. A long-time pilgrimage site, the town's 12th- to 13th-century **church** venerates the spot where St Martin died in 397. Wander down to the benches overlooking the waterfront along rue du Confluent (a pleasant spot for a picnic), or follow the brown 'Panorama Piétons' signs above the church for higher-altitude perspectives.

The Drive » Snake 6km south along the D751, D7 and D947, following signs for Fontevraud-l'Abbaye. From the D7/D947 junction, a worthwhile 800m detour leads northwest to the artisanal soap factory Savonnerie Martin de Candre.

- - - - - - - - - - - -

⑤ Abbaye de Fontevraud (p83)

This huge 12th-century **complex** (☎02 41 51 73 52; www.abbayedefontevraud.com; adult/child €9.50/7, audioguide €4.50, smartphone app free; ☺9.30am-6.30pm Apr-mid–Nov, 10am-5.30pm Tue-Sat mid-Nov–Mar, closed Jan) was once one of Europe's largest ecclesiastical centres. The highlight here is the massive, movingly simple **abbey church**, notable for its soaring pillars, Romanesque domes and the polychrome,tombs of four Plantagenets: Henry II, King of England (r 1154–89); his wife Eleanor of Aquitaine (who retired to Fontevraud after Henry's death); their son Richard the Lionheart; and Isabelle of Angoulème. Adjacent buildings include a cavernous, multi-chimneyed kitchen, prayer halls, a barrel-vaulted refectory and exhibits on Fontevraud's use as a prison from the French Revolution until 1963.

The Drive » Backtrack 5km to the D751 and follow it 13km southeast toward Chinon. Immediately after crossing the Vienne River, take the D749 east 3km, paralleling the riverfront into town.

Cobblestoned street, Chinon

TRIP HIGHLIGHT

⑥ Chinon (p77)

Renowned for its hilltop château and charming medieval quarter (see our walking tour, p36), the riverside village of Chinon is home to several fine restaurants and AOC red wines, making it a prime candidate for an overnight stay. For customised half-day tours of nearby wine-growing regions, including Chinon, Cravant, Saumur-Champigny, St-Nicolas-de-Bourgeuil and Touraine, contact bilingual Chinon native **Alain Caillemer** (☏02 47 95 87 59; dcaillemer@rand.com; half-day tours per couple €75).

The Drive ❯❯ Zigzag 8km southwest of Chinon through lovely rolling farmland along the D749A, D751E, D759, D24 and D117, following signs for La Devinière.

⑦ Musée Rabelais

Set among fields and vineyards with sweeping views to the private château of Coudray Montpensier, **La Devinière** is the birthplace of François Rabelais – doctor, Franciscan friar, theoretician and author – and the inspiration for his five satirical Gargantua and Pantagruel novels. The farmstead's rambling buildings hold the **Musée**

33

Rabelais (www.musee-rabelais.fr; adult/child €5/4; ◷10am-12.30pm & 2-5pm daily, closed Tue Oct-Mar), featuring early editions of Rabelais' work and a Matisse portrait of the author. The winding cave network underneath hosts rotating special exhibitions.

The Drive » Follow the D117 8km west through the gorgeous village of Seuilly, home to an 11th-century abbey, then continue 13km west-northwest along the D48, D50, D310, D110 and D93 into Brézé.

⑧ Château de Brézé (p85)

Off-the-beaten-track **Château de Brézé** (www.chateaudebreze.com; adult/child €11/6; ◷10am-6.30pm Apr-Sep, to 7.30 Jul & Aug, to 6pm Tue-Sun Oct-Mar, closed Jan) sits atop an extensive network of subterranean rooms and passages that account for more square footage than the castle itself. A self-guided tour takes you through the original troglodyte dwelling directly under the château, then crosses a deep moat to other caves adapted by the castle's owners for use as kitchens, wine cellars and defensive bastions. Finish your visit with a scenic climb to the château's rooftop, followed by a *dégustation* (tasting) of Saumur wines from the surrounding vineyards.

The Drive » Chart a meandering 22km course

through relatively flat farm country into Doué-la-Fontaine via the D93, D162, D163 and D960.

⑨ Doué-la-Fontaine (p84)

At the southeastern edge of this mid-sized town, stop to visit the fascinating **Troglodytes et Sarcophages** (www.troglo-sarcophages.fr; adult/child €4.80/3.30; ◷2.30-7pm daily Jun-Sep, Sat & Sun May), a Merovingian quarry where sarcophagi were produced from the 6th to the 9th centuries and exported via the Loire as far as England and Belgium. In summer book ahead for atmospheric lantern-lit evening **tours** (adult/child €7.50/5.50).

Near by, **Les Perrières** (www.les-perrieres.fr; adult/child €4.50/3; ◷2-6.30pm Tue-Sun Apr-Oct) is a vast network of 18th- and 19th-century stone quarries sometimes called the 'cathedral caves' due to their lofty sloping walls that resemble Gothic arches.

The Drive » Skirt the southern edge of Doué-la-Fontaine via the D960 for 4km, then continue 5km north on the D761 to the Rochemenier exit. Follow signs the remaining 1.5km into Rochemenier.

TRIP HIGHLIGHT

⑩ Rochemenier (p84)

In peaceful countryside northwest of Doué-la-Fontaine, the museum-

village of **Rochemenier** (www.troglodyte.info; adult/child €5.90/3.50; ◷9.30am-6pm Apr-Sep, 10am-5pm Tue-Sun Oct-Nov, Feb & Mar) preserves the remains of two troglodyte farmsteads that were inhabited until the 1930s, complete with houses, stables and an underground chapel. Throughout the complex, farm tools and photos of former residents evoke the hard-working spirit and simple pleasures that defined life underground for many generations. Displays in the last room focus on international cave-dwelling cultures, including places as far-flung as China and Turkey.

The Drive » Return to the D761, then follow it 15km northwest to Brissac-Quincé, where signs direct you 1.5km further to the château.

⑪ Château de Brissac (p88)

France's tallest castle, the imposing **Château de Brissac** (www.chateau-brissac.fr; guided tours adult/child €10/4.50; ◷10am-12.15pm & 2-6pm Wed-Mon Apr-Oct, 10am-6pm Jul & Aug) is spread over seven storeys and 204 rooms. Built by the Duke of Brissac in 1502, the château has an elegant interior filled with posh furniture, ornate tapestries, twinkling chandeliers and luxurious bedrooms – even a private theatre.

DETOUR:
ANGERS (P85)

Start ⑪ Château de Brissac

Historic seat of Anjou's powerful counts and dukes, bustling Angers revolves around the impressive **Château d'Angers** (angers.monuments-nationaux.fr; 2 promenade du Bout-du-Monde; adult/child €8.50/free; ⊙9.30am-6.30pm May-Aug, 10am-5.30pm Sep-Apr). The castle's walls of blue-black schist loom above the Maine River, ringed by gardens, battlements and 17 watchtowers. Inside is one of Europe's great medieval masterpieces, the **Tenture de l'Apocalypse**. Commissioned around 1375, this stunning 104m-long series of tapestries illustrates scenes from the Book of Revelation, complete with the Four Horsemen of the Apocalypse, the Battle of Armageddon and the seven-headed Beast.

Opposite the château, taste and learn about the region's well-regarded wines at the **Maison du Vin de l'Anjou** (mdesvins-angers@vinsdeloire.fr; 5bis place du Président Kennedy; ⊙2.30-7pm Mon, 10am-1pm & 2.30-7pm Tue-Sat). Afterwards stroll through Angers' pedestrianised centre, where you'll find cafes, restaurants, art museums and the fabulous **Maison d'Adam** (place Ste-Croix), a remarkably well-preserved medieval house decorated with bawdy carved figurines.

To get here, head 28km northwest from Brissac on the D748, A87 and A11, following signs for Angers-Centre.

Around the house, 8 sq km of grounds are filled with cedar trees, 19th-century stables and a vineyard, boasting three AOC vintages; free tastings are included in the guided visit.

The Drive » Follow the D55 6km northeast, then wind 15km east-southeast on the D751 through forests and sunflower fields to rejoin the Loire at Gennes. From here, a particularly scenic stretch of the D751 follows the Loire's sandy banks 12km to St-Hilaire-St-Florent. Along the way, the small towns of St-Georges-des-Sept-Voies (p155) and Chênehutte-Trèves-Cunault (p155) offer enticing eating and sleeping options.

⑫ St-Hilaire-St-Florent (p84)

This western suburb of Saumur is crowded with wineries and cave-based attractions. At the **Musée du Champignon** (Mushroom Museum; www.musee-du-champignon.com; D751; adult/child €8/6; ⊙10am-6pm Feb, Mar, Oct & Nov, to 7pm Apr-Sep), learn oodles of mushroom facts and trivia as you wander deep into a cave where countless varieties of fungi are cultivated; next door, **Pierre et Lumière** (www.pierre-et-lumiere.com; D751; adult/child €8/6; ⊙10am-7pm Apr-Sep, to

12.30pm & 2-6pm Feb, Mar, Oct & Nov) displays intricate limestone sculptures of famous Loire Valley monuments. East towards Saumur, a host of tasting rooms invites you to sample local AOC and AOP vintages including Crémant de Loire and Saumur Brut; well-established wineries along this route include **Ackerman** (www.ackerman.fr), **Gratien et Meyer** (www.gratienmeyer.com), **Langlois Château** (www.langlois-chateau.fr) and **Veuve Amiot** (www.veuveamiot.fr).

The Drive » A quick 3km scoot along the D751 and D161 returns you to downtown Saumur.

STRETCH YOUR LEGS
CHINON

Start/Finish
Hostellerie Gargantua

Distance 3km

Duration Three hours

This relaxed walk leads you through Chinon's medieval centre from one end to the other, visiting both the lower town and the historic castle above, culminating in a scenic stroll along the cave-riddled cliff face to the east.

Take this walk on Trips

Hostellerie Gargantua

Renowned author François Rabelais (c 1483–1553) grew up in Chinon; this atmospheric **hotel** (73 rue Haute St-Maurice), housed in a Gothic palace that once served as headquarters for the king's representative in Chinon, is one of several places bearing Rabelais-related names that you'll find scattered throughout the old town. On the same street, look for the **Hôtel du Gouverneur**, an impressive town house with a double-flighted staircase ensconced behind a carved gateway.

The Walk » Head east a few paces along rue Haute St-Maurice to the museum on the opposite side of the street.

Musée d'Art et d'Histoire

This small municipal **museum** (44 rue Haute St-Maurice; adult/child €3/free; ⊙2.30-6.30pm Wed-Mon May–mid-Sep, 2-6pm Fri-Mon mid-Sep–mid-Nov & mid-Feb–Apr, closed mid-Nov–mid-Feb) has a collection of Chinon-related art and archaeological finds dating from prehistory to the 19th century, including a painting of Rabelais by Delacroix. Outside the museum is the intersection of two medieval streets, whose half-timbered buildings are said to have housed Joan of Arc while she awaited her audience with the dauphin Charles.

The Walk » Continue east along rue Haute St-Maurice, which soon changes its name to rue Voltaire. Look for the Caves Painctes de Chinon in the cliff face to your left.

Caves Painctes de Chinon

Hidden at the end of a cobbled alleyway off rue Voltaire are the **Caves Painctes de Chinon** (impasse des Caves Painctes; adult/child €3/free; ⊙guided tours 11am, 3pm, 4.30pm & 6pm Tue-Sun Jul & Aug), a network of former quarries that were converted into wine cellars during the 15th century. Local winegrowers run tours of the *caves* (wine cellars) in summer.

The Walk » Return to rue Voltaire, then walk diagonally across the street to La Cave Voltaire.

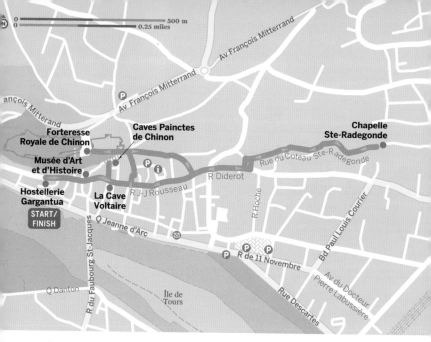

La Cave Voltaire

A great place for a mid-afternoon snack or an evening drink, **La Cave Voltaire** (www.lacavevoltaire.fr; 13 rue Voltaire) stocks over 200 wines from the Chinon region and beyond. Tasty platters of local cheese and charcuterie are served with hearty fresh bread at pavement tables with nice views up to Chinon's castle.

The Walk ≫ Follow rue Voltaire three blocks east into Chinon's picturesque main square, place du Général de Gaulle, then turn left (uphill) two blocks and take the free elevator to the upper town. Once up top, turn left and climb to the castle.

Forteresse Royale de Chinon

Chinon's star attraction is this fabulous **castle** (www.forteressechinon.fr; adult/child €7.50/5.50; 9.30am-7pm May-Aug, to 5pm or 6pm rest of year). The 12th-century **Fort St-Georges** and **Logis Royal** (Royal Lodgings) date from the Plantagenet court of Henry II and Eleanor of Aquitaine, while the 14th-century **Tour de l'Horloge** (Clock Tower) houses exhibits commemorating Joan of Arc's

1429 meeting with the future Charles VII. For stupendous panoramas, climb atop the 13th-century **Fort du Coudray**.

The Walk ≫ Descend rue du Puy des Bancs to rue Jean-Jacques Rousseau, turn left and continue two blocks to St-Mexme church. Climb left of the church on rue de Pitoche, then follow rue du Coteau Ste-Radegonde 500m past cave-pockmarked cliffs to Chapelle Ste-Radegonde.

Chapelle Ste-Radegonde

Surrounded by abandoned troglodyte dwellings, this mystical, half-ruined medieval **chapel** (rue du Coteau Ste-Radegonde; adult/child €3/free; 3-6pm Sat & Sun May, Jun & Sep, 3-6pm Wed-Mon Jul & Aug) is built partly into a cave, accessed by a red door in an old stone wall. The chapel's 12th-century 'Royal Hunt' fresco is said to represent members of the Plantagenet royal family; inside, a staircase descends to a subterranean spring associated with a pre-Christian cult.

The Walk ≫ Retrace your steps to Hostellerie Gargantua via St-Mexme church, rue Jean-Jacques Rousseau and place du Général de Gaulle.

37

Medieval Burgundy

3

Fortified hill towns, medieval monasteries, exquisite Romanesque capitals and multicoloured tiled roofs share the stage with rolling vineyards and verdant hiking trails on this idyllic meander.

TRIP HIGHLIGHTS

Noyers-sur-Serein

6

216 km

Abbaye de Fontenay
Tranquil end-of-the-road domain of 12th-century Cistercian monks

Semur-en-Auxois

8 FINISH

81 km

Beaune
Burgundy's wine capital, crowned by kaleidoscopic roof tiles

Autun

3

Tournus

1 START

Vézelay
A hilltop treasury of Romanesque architecture

327 km

Cluny
Once Christendom's grandest abbey, reduced to peaceful ruins

0 km

---

6 DAYS
327KM / 203 MILES

GREAT FOR...

BEST TIME TO GO
From May wildflower season through to the October wine harvest.

 ESSENTIAL PHOTO
Vézelay's sinuous sweep of stone houses crowned by a hilltop basilica.

 BEST FOR OUTDOORS
The riverside walking trails around Noyers-sur-Serein.

top village of Vézelay (p45)

39

3 Medieval Burgundy

Between the Middle Ages and the 15th century, Burgundy saw a tremendous flowering of ecclesiastical architecture, from Cistercian and Benedictine monasteries to Romanesque basilicas, coupled with active patronage of the arts by the powerful Dukes of Burgundy. This medieval meander shows you all the highlights, while mixing in opportunities for wine tasting and walking in the gorgeous rolling countryside that makes Burgundy one of France's most appealing regions.

TRIP HIGHLIGHT

❶ Cluny (p103)

Built between 1088 and 1130, the monumental Benedictine **Abbaye de Cluny** (cluny. monuments-nationaux. fr; adult/child €9.50/free; ☺9.30am-6pm Apr-Sep, to 7pm Jul & Aug, to 5pm Oct-Mar) – Christendom's largest church until the construction of St Peter's in Rome – once held sway over 1400 monasteries stretching from Poland to Portugal. Today you'll need a good imagination to conjure up the abbey's 12th-century glory, but its fragmentary remains, bordered by the giant shade trees of the grassy **Parc Abbatial** are a delightful place to wander.

Get oriented at the **Musée d'Art et d'Archéologie** (combined ticket with Église Abbatiale adult/child €9.50/free; ☺9.30am-7pm Jul & Aug, to 6pm Apr-Jun & Sep, to 5pm Oct-Mar), with its scale model of the Cluny complex and 3-D 'virtual tour' of the abbey's original medieval layout, then climb the **Tour des**

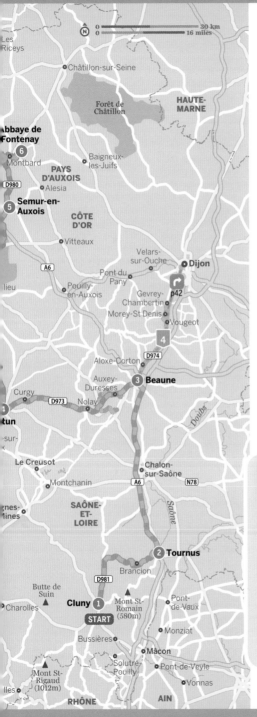

Fromages (adult/child €2/ free; ⏰9.30am-12.30pm & 2.30-6pm, no midday closure Jul & Aug, closed Sun Nov-Mar) for a bird's-eye view of the abbey's remains, including the striking octagonal **Clocher de l'Eau Bénite** (Tower of the Holy Water) and the **Farinier** (Granary), where eight splendid capitals from the original church are displayed.

The Drive ≫ Head 13km north along the D981 to Cormatin, with its Renaissance-style château, then squiggle 25km east along the D14 past Chapaize's 11th-century Église St-Martin, Ozenay's château and the medieval hill town of Brancion before descending into Tournus.

- - - - - - - - - - - - - -

② Tournus (p103)

Tournus' superb 10th- to 12th-century Benedictine abbey, **Abbatiale St-Philibert** (⏰8.30am-6pm, to 7pm in summer),

LINK YOUR TRIP

1 Châteaux of the Loire

Three hours west of Vézelay, explore the Loire Valley's classic châteaux.

4 Route des Grands Crus

Switch gears in Beaune to discover Burgundy's best wines.

41

makes a striking first impression, with its austere Romanesque facade peeking out through a medieval stone gate flanked by twin rounded towers; its apse holds an extremely rare 12th-century **floor mosaic** of the calendar and the zodiac, discovered by chance in 2002. The medieval centre also boasts fine restaurants – good for a lunch stop.

The Drive » From Tournus, zip 56km straight up the A6 to Beaune.

TRIP HIGHLIGHT

3 Beaune (p93)

Burgundy's prosperous and supremely appealing viticultural capital, Beaune, is surrounded by vineyards producing an impressive array of appellations including

Côte de Nuits and Côte de Beaune. Sipping local vintages at sunset on a cafe terrace here is one of France's great pleasures. For a grand tour of the region's renowned wineries, see p47.

The architectural jewel of Beaune's historic centre is the **Hôtel-Dieu des Hospices de Beaune** (www.hospices-de-beaune. com; rue de l'Hôtel-Dieu; adult/child €7/3; ☺9am-6.30pm), a 15th-century charity hospital topped by stunning turrets and pitched rooftops covered in multicoloured tiles. Interior highlights include the barrel-vaulted **Grande Salle** with its dragon-embellished beams; an 18th-century **pharmacy** lined with ancient flasks; and the multipanelled 15th-century Flemish

masterpiece **Polyptych of the Last Judgement**.

The Drive » A super-scenic 49km drive along the D973 weaves southwest through gorgeous vineyard country, climbing past La Rochepot's striking 13th-century castle before turning due west to Autun.

4 Autun (p101)

Two millennia ago, Autun (Augustodunum) was one of Roman Gaul's most important cities. Its next heyday came 1100 years later, when **Cathédrale St-Lazare** (place du Terreau; ☺8am-7pm Sep-Jun, plus 9-11pm Jul & Aug; chapter room summer months only) was built to house St Lazarus' sacred relics. Climb through the old city's narrow cobblestone streets to see the cathedral's fantastical Romanesque capitals

---

DETOUR:
DIJON

Start 3 **Beaune**

Long-time capital of medieval Burgundy, Dijon was the seat of power for a series of enlightened dukes who presided over the region's 14th- and 15th-century golden age, filling the city with fine art and architecture. From Beaune follow the D974 42km north through the vineyards into downtown Dijon, then park and explore the city's treasures on foot.

Topping the list of must-see attractions are the 13th-century **Église Notre Dame** (place Notre-Dame) with its remarkable facade of pencil-thin columns and leering gargoyles; the **Palais des Ducs et des États de Bourgogne** (place de la Libération), the Burgundy dukes' monumental palace, which also houses Dijon's superb art museum, the **Musée des Beaux-Arts** (mba.dijon.fr; tours adult/child €6/3; ☺10am-5pm Wed-Mon); and the **historic mansions** that line surrounding streets, especially rue des Forges, rue Verrerie, rue Vannerie and rue de la Chouette.

For complete coverage of this engaging city, see Lonely Planet's *France* guide.

Hôtel-Dieu des Hospices de Beaune

and famous 12th-century **tympanum** depicting the Last Judgement, carved by Burgundy's master sculptor Gislebertus. Across the street, the **Musée Rolin** (5 rue des Bancs; adult/child €5/free; ⏰9.30am-noon & 1.30-6pm Wed-Mon) houses Gislebertus' precociously sensual masterpiece, the *Temptation of Eve*, alongside Gallo-Roman artefacts and modern paintings.

Roman treasures around town include the town gates **Porte d'Arroux** and **Porte St-André**, the 16,000-seat **Théâtre Romain**, the **Temple de Janus** and the **Pierre de Couhard**, a 27m-high remnant of a Gallo-Roman pyramid.

Autun makes an excellent base for exploring the nearby **Parc Naturel Régional du Morvan** (www.parcdumorvan. org); the park's website offers downloadable hiking, biking and equestrian itineraries.

The Drive » The D980 runs 70km north from Autun to Semur-en-Auxois; halfway along, there's a fine collection of Romanesque capitals at Saulieu's 12th-century Basilique de St-Andoche.

- - - - - - - - - - - -

5 Semur-en-Auxois

Perched on a granite spur, surrounded by a hairpin turn in the Armançon River and guarded by four massive pink-granite bastions, Semur-en-Auxois was once an important

Serein River, Noyers-sur-Serein

religious centre boasting no fewer than six monasteries.

Pass through the two concentric medieval gates, **Porte Sauvigne** and **Porte Guillier**, onto pedestrianised rue Buffon, where you can sample a few *semurettes* (local dark-chocolate truffles) at **Pâtisserie Coeur** (les-semurettes.com; 14 rue Buffon; ☺8am-7pm Tue-Sun) before continuing west to Promenade du Rempart for panoramic views from atop Semur's medieval battlements.

Semur is especially atmospheric at night, when the ramparts are illuminated, and around Pentecost, when the **Fêtes Médiévales du Roi Chaussé** fill the streets with medieval-themed parades and markets.

The Drive ≫ Follow the D980 20km north into Montbard, then hop 2km east on the D905 before joining the sleepy northbound D32 for the idyllic 3km home stretch into Fontenay.

- - - - - - - - - - - -

TRIP HIGHLIGHT

❻ Abbaye de Fontenay

Founded in 1118 and restored to its medieval glory a century ago, the Unesco-listed **Abbaye de Fontenay** (www. abbayedefontenay.com; adult/child €9.50/5.50, incl guided tour €11.50/6.50; ☺10am-noon & 2-5pm) offers a fascinating glimpse of the austere, serene surroundings in which Cistercian monks lived lives of contemplation, prayer and manual labour. Set in a bucolic wooded valley, the abbey includes an unadorned Romanesque church, a barrel-vaulted monks' dormitory, landscaped gardens and Europe's first metallurgical factory, with a remarkable water-driven forge from 1220.

From the parking lot, the GR213 trail forms part of two verdant walking circuits: one to Montbard (13km return), the other (11.5km) through Touillon and Le Petit Jailly. Maps and botanical field guides are available in the abbey shop.

The Drive ≫ Backtrack to the D905, follow it 14km west-northwest to Rougemont, then take the westbound D956 21km into Noyers.

❼ Noyers-sur-Serein (p98)

Tucked into a sharp bend in the Serein River, picturesque medieval Noyers is surrounded by pastureland and wooded hills. The town's cobbled streets, accessed via two imposing stone gateways, lead past 15th- and 16th-century gabled houses, wood and stone archways and several art galleries.

Noyers is a superb base for walking. Just outside the clock-topped southern gate, **Chemin des Fossés** threads its way between the Serein and the village's 13th-century fortifications, 19 of whose original 23 towers still remain. The 9km **Balade du Château**, marked in red, follows the Serein's right bank past an utterly ruined château.

In summer, the **Rencontres Musicales de Noyers** (www. musicalesdenoyers.com) bring classical concerts and jazz sessions to town.

The Drive » Snake 14km southward through the peaceful Serein valley via the D86, then head 11km west on the D11 from Dissangis to Joux-la-Ville before charting a southwest course down the D32, D9, D606 and D951 for the final 24km run into Vézelay.

TRIP HIGHLIGHT

❽ Vézelay (p99)

Rising from lush rolling countryside and crowned by a venerable medieval basilica, Vézelay is one of France's loveliest hilltop villages. Founded in the 9th century on a former Roman and then Carolingian site, the magnificent **Basilique Ste-Madeleine** (www. basiliquedevezelay.org) gained early fame as a starting point for the Santiago de Compostela pilgrimage route. Among its treasures are a 12th-century **tympanum**, with a carving of an enthroned Jesus radiating his holy spirit to the Apostles; several beautifully carved Romanesque **capitals**, including the Mystical Mill, which depicts Moses grinding grain into a flour sack held by St Paul; and a mid-12th-century **crypt** reputed to house one of Mary Magdalene's bones. Concerts of sacred music are held here from June to September.

The **park** behind the basilica affords wonderful views and walking access to the verdant Vallée de Cure. From **Porte Neuve**, Vézelay's old town gate, a footpath descends via the 12th-century chapel of **La Cordelle** to the village of **Asquins**. Another nice walk is the **Promenade des Fossés**, which circumnavigates Vézelay's medieval ramparts.

Route des Grands Crus

4

The picture-book Route des Grands Crus laces together Burgundy's most reputed vineyards. And, yes, opportunities abound for pleasurable wine tasting in historic surrounds.

TRIP HIGHLIGHTS

7 km

Château du Clos de Vougeot
A magnificent wine-growing estate

29 km

Beaune
The opulent capital of Burgundian wines

Pommard

39 km

Château de La Rochepot

Puligny-Montrachet

Château de Meursault
Wine tasting in a grandiose setting

St-Romain
Sensational views and a bucolic atmosphere

45 km

START
Gevrey-Chambertin

Nuits-St-Georges

FINISH

2 DAYS
62KM / 38 MILES

GREAT FOR...

BEST TIME TO GO

May, June, September and October for a symphony of colour and quiet roads.

ESSENTIAL PHOTO

The views from the cliffs that tower above St-Romain are hallucinogenic.

BEST FOR FOODIES

Beaune is a great place to try Burgundian specialities like snails.

ard worker inspects pinot noir grapes, Burgundy

4 Route des Grands Crus

Swinging from Gevrey-Chambertin to Puligny-Montrachet, this route is like a 'greatest hits' of Burgundy, with its bucolic views, patchwork of immaculate hand-groomed vines, atmospheric wine cellars and attractive stone villages. If you're looking for an upscale wine château experience, you've come to the right place. Now is your chance to sample some of the most prestigious reds and whites in the world.

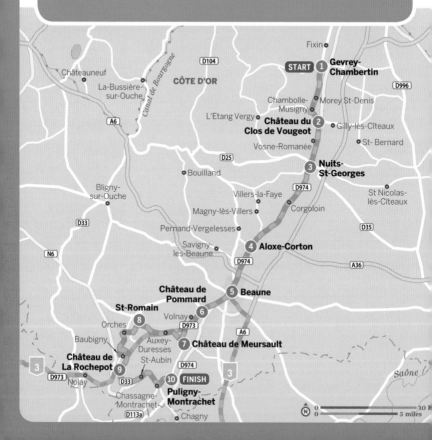

❶ Gevrey-Chambertin

Kick-start your epicurean adventure by visiting this picturesque village, which enjoys a world-class reputation among wine enthusiasts – it produces nine out of the 32 Grands Crus wines from Burgundy. All are reds made from pinot noir.

The Drive » From Gevrey-Chambertin it's a relaxed drive along the D122 to Château du Clos de Vougeot, 7km south via Morey St-Denis and Chambolle-Musigny.

TRIP HIGHLIGHT

❷ Château du Clos de Vougeot (p90)

An essential stop on the Route des Grands Crus, the magnificent wine-producing **Château du Clos de Vougeot** (www.closdevougeot.fr; Vougeot; adult/child €7/2.50; ⊙9am-6.30pm Apr-Oct, 10am-5pm Nov-Mar, closes 5pm Sat year-round) is regarded as the

LINK YOUR TRIP

3 Medieval Burgundy

It's easy to combine this trip with our itinerary focusing on medieval Burgundy, either from Beaune or La Rochepot.

birthplace of Burgundian wines. Originally the property of the Abbaye de Cîteaux, 12km southeast from here, the 16th-century country castle served as a getaway for the monks who stored their equipment and produced their wines here for several centuries. Tours uncover the workings of enormous wine presses and casks.

The Drive » Pick up the D974 to Nuits-St-Georges, 4.5km south via Vosne-Romanée.

❸ Nuits-St-Georges (p89)

It's worth spending a little time in attractive Nuits-St-Georges. Splashed around town are a dozen domaines selling superb reds and whites, but an essential port of call on any wine-tasting itinerary is **L'Imaginarium** (www.imaginariumbourgogne.com; av du Jura; adult/child €8/5; ⊙2-7pm Mon, 10am-7pm Tue-Sun). This gleaming modern museum is a great place to learn about Burgundy wines and winemaking techniques. It's fun and entertaining, with movies, exhibits and interactive displays.

Architecture buffs should take a look at the appealing 17th-century **belfry** of the former town hall and the Romanesque **Église St-Symphorien**,

slightly away from the town centre.

The Drive » Continue along the D974 towards Beaune. After passing through the village of Ladoix-Serrigny, look out for the sign to Château Corton-André on the right. It's a 10-minute drive from Nuits-St-Georges (11.5km).

❹ Aloxe-Corton (p92)

Surrounded by manicured vineyards, tiny Aloxe-Corton is a real charmer. It's great for wine lovers, with producers handily scattered around the village. A good starting point is **Domaines d'Aloxe-Corton** (place du Chapitre; ⊙10am-1pm & 3-7pm Thu-Mon Apr–mid-Nov), a polished wine shop representing several makers of the terrific Aloxe-Corton *appellation* (delectable reds and whites).

No visit to Aloxe-Corton would be complete without visiting the high-flying **Château Corton-André** (☎03 80 26 28 79; www.pierre-andre.com; ⊙10am-1pm & 2.30-6pm). With its splendid cellars and tiled roofs, it's a wonderful place for a tasting session in atmospheric surrounds.

The Drive » Pick up the busy N74 to Beaune, 5.5km due south.

❺ Beaune (p93)

Beaune's *raison d'être* and the source of its *joie de vivre* is wine: making it, tasting it, selling it, but most of all, drinking it. Consequently Beaune is one of the best places in all of France for wine tasting.

The amoeba-shaped old city is enclosed by thick stone **ramparts**, which are lined with overgrown gardens and ringed by a pathway that makes for a lovely stroll.

The most striking attraction of Beaune's old city is the magnificent **Hôtel-Dieu des Hospices de Beaune** (see p93).

Underneath Beaune's buildings, streets and ramparts, millions of dusty bottles of wine are being aged to perfection in cool, dark cellars. The bacchanalian **Marché aux Vins** (www.marcheauxvins.com; 2 rue Nicolas Rolin; admission €10; ⏰9.30-11.30am & 2-5.30pm Sep-Jun, 9.30am-5.30pm Jul & Aug) is a one-stop shop to taste, learn about and buy Burgundy wines. Using a *tastevin* (a small silver cup), sample an impressive 15 wines in the candle-lit former Église des Cordeliers and its cellars. Another venerable winery is **Bouchard Père & Fils** (www.bouchard-pereetfils.com; 15 rue du Château; ⏰10am-12.30pm & 2.30-6.30pm Mon-Sat, 10am-12.30pm Sun Apr-Nov, 10am-12.30pm & 2.30-5.30pm Mon-Sat Dec-Mar), housed in a medieval fortress.

ESCARGOTS

One of France's trademark culinary habits, the consumption of gastropod molluscs – preferably with butter, garlic, parsley and fresh bread – is inextricably linked in the public mind with Burgundy because *Helix pomatia,* though endemic in much of Europe, is best known as *escargot de Bourgogne* (the Burgundy snail). Once a regular, and unwelcome, visitor to the fine-wine vines of Burgundy and a staple on Catholic plates during Lent, the humble hermaphroditic crawler has been decimated by overharvesting and the use of agricultural chemicals, and is now a protected species. As a result, the vast majority of the critters impaled on French snail forks (the ones with two tongs) are now imported from Turkey, Greece and Eastern Europe.

The Drive ⟩⟩ Take the D974 (direction Autun), then the D973 to Pommard (5.5km).

❻ Château de Pommard (p92)

For many red wine lovers, a visit to the superb **Château de Pommard** (www.chateaudepommard.com; 15 rue Marey-Monge; guided tours incl tasting adult/child €21/free; ⏰9.30am-6pm Apr-Nov) is the ultimate Burgundian pilgrimage. The impressive cellars contain many vintage bottles.

The Drive ⟩⟩ Follow signs to Meursault (5km), via Volnay. Château de Meursault is signposted in the centre of the village.

❼ Château de Meursault (p92)

One of the most elegant of the Route des Grands Crus châteaux, **Château de Meursault** (www.chateau-meursault.com; rue Moulin-Foulot; admission incl tasting €18; ⏰10am-noon & 2-6pm Mar, Apr, Oct & Nov, 10am-6.30pm May-Sep, 10am-noon & 2-6pm Sat, 10am-1pm Sun Feb) has beautiful grounds and produces prestigious white wines. You'll be struck by the 14th-century cellars.

The Drive ⟩⟩ From the centre of Meursault, follow signs to Auxey-Duresses and Nolay (D23), then signs to Auxey-Duresses and St-Romain (D17E).

Château de La Rochepot (p52)

Then take the D973 (direction Auxey-Duresses). Leaving Auxey-Duresses, take the D17E to Auxey-le-Petit and St-Romain (6.5km from Meursault).

TRIP HIGHLIGHT

8 St-Romain

Off-the-beaten-path St-Romain is a bucolic village situated right where vineyards meet pastureland, forests and cliffs. For drop-dead views over the village and the valley, drive up to the panoramic viewpoint (it's signposted), which is perched atop a cliff near the ruins of a castle.

The Drive » Pass through St-Romain and follow signs to Falaises along the D17, then turn left onto the D17 (direction Falaises, Orches, Baubigny). It's a lovely drive with scenic vistas until you reach Baubigny. In Baubigny take the D111D to La Rochepot. It's an 8km drive from Meursault.

9 Château de La Rochepot (p92)

With its conical towers and multicoloured tile roofs rising from thick woods above the ancient village of La Rochepot, the **Château de La Rochepot** (www. larochepot.com; La Rochepot; adult/child €4.50/2.50; ☺10am-noon & 2-5.30pm Wed-Sun) is a dream come true for photographers

---

BURGUNDY WINE BASICS

Burgundy's epic vineyards extend approximately 258km from Chablis in the north to the Rhône's Beaujolais in the south and comprise 100 Appellations d'Origine Contrôlée (AOC). Each region has its own appellations and traits, embodied by a concept called *terroir* – the earth imbuing its produce, such as grapes, with unique qualities.

Here's an ever-so-brief survey of some of Burgundy's major growing regions:

Côte d'Or vineyards The northern section, the Côte de Nuits, stretches from Marsannay-la-Côte (near Dijon) south to Corgoloin and produces reds known for their robust, full-bodied character. The southern section, the Côte de Beaune, lies between Ladoix-Serrigny and Santenay and produces great reds and great whites. Appellations from the area's hilltops are the Hautes-Côtes de Nuits and Hautes-Côtes de Beaune.

Chablis & Grand Auxerrois Four renowned chardonnay white-wine appellations from 20 villages around Chablis. Part of the Auxerrois vineyards, Irancy produces excellent pinot noir reds.

Châtillonnais Approximately 20 villages around Châtillon-sur-Seine producing red and white wines.

Côte Chalonnaise The southernmost continuation of the Côte de Beaune's slopes is noted for its excellent reds and whites.

Mâconnais Known for rich or fruity white wines, like the Pouilly-Fuissé chardonnay.

Want to Know More?
Take a class!

École des Vins de Bourgogne (☏03 80 26 35 10; www.ecoledesvins-bourgogne.com; 6 rue du 16e Chasseurs, Beaune) Offers a variety of courses.

Sensation Vin (☏03 80 22 17 57; www.sensation-vin.com; 1 rue d'Enfer, Beaune; ☺10am-7pm) Offers introductory tasting sessions (no appointment needed) as well as tailor-made courses.

Grapes ripening in the sun

and history buffs. This marvellous medieval fortress offers fab views of surrounding countryside.

The Drive » Look for the D973 (direction Nolay); after 200m look for the left-hand turn onto the D33 that plunges down to St-Aubin. In St-Aubin turn left onto the D906 (direction Chagny), and eventually turn left onto the D113A to Puligny-Montrachet (10km from La Rochepot). It's a journey of 10km.

⑩ Puligny-Montrachet (p92)

Puligny-Montrachet makes a grand finale to your trip. Beloved of white wine aficionados (no reds in sight), this bijou appellation is revered thanks to five extraordinary Grands Crus. At the **Caveau de Puligny-Montrachet**

(📞03 80 21 96 78; www. caveau-puligny.com; 1 rue de Poiseul; 🕙9.30am-noon & 2-8pm Mar-Oct) you can sample various local wines in a comfortable and relaxed setting. This wine bar–cellar is run by knowledgeable Julien Wallerand, who provides excellent advice (in decent English).

Destinations

Loire Valley (p56)
If it's pomp and splendour you're looking for, explore the châteaux, villages and vineyards of the Loire Valley.

Burgundy (p89)
Burgundy entices with its world-class vineyards, rolling green hills and medieval villages.

Château d'Azay-le-Rideau (p76)
LIONEL LOURDEL/GETTY IMAGES ©

Loire Valley

Sprinkled with many of the most extravagant castles and fortresses in France, the Loire Valley is jam-packed with astonishingly rich architectural, artistic and agrarian treasures.

History

The dramas of French history are writ large across the face of the Loire Valley's châteaux. Early on, the Loire was one of Roman Gaul's most important transport arteries. The first châteaux were medieval fortresses established in the 9th century to fend off marauding Vikings. By the 11th century massive walls, fortified keeps and moats were all the rage.

During the Hundred Years War (1337–1453) the Loire marked one of the boundaries between French and English forces and the area was ravaged by fierce fighting. After Charles VII regained his crown with the help of Joan of Arc, the Loire emerged as the centre of French court life. Charles took up residence in Loches with his mistress, Agnès Sorel, and the French nobility, and from then on the bourgeois elite established their own extravagant châteaux as expressions of wealth and influence.

François I (r 1515–47) made his mark by introducing ornate Renaissance palaces to the Loire. François' successor Henri II (r 1547–59), his wife Catherine de Médici and his mistress Diane de Poitiers played out their interpersonal dramas from castle to castle, while Henri's son, Henri III (r 1573–89), had two of his greatest rivals assassinated at Blois' Castle before being assassinated himself eight months later.

❶ Getting There & Away

AIR

Tours' airport has flights to London's Stansted, Southampton (England), Dublin (Ireland), Marseille, Marrakesh (Morocco) and Porto (Portugal), while Angers' small airport serves London and Nice.

TRAIN

The TGV connects St-Pierre-des-Corps, 4km east of Tours, with Paris' Gare Montparnasse (one hour) and Charles de Gaulle Airport (1¾ hour); in the west, Saumur, Angers and Nantes; and in the south, La Rochelle and Bordeaux. Angers is also on the TGV line via Le Mans to Paris. Blois and Amboise are served by high-speed trains to Paris. Some châteaux are on or near regional lines.

❶ Getting Around

Most main towns and many châteaux are accessible by train or bus, but having your own wheels allows significantly more freedom.

Blois has decent public buses and shuttles to nearby châteaux. Tours and Amboise are loaded with bus tour options.

BICYCLE

The mostly flat Loire Valley is fabulous cycling country – peddle through villages and vineyards on your way to châteaux. **Loire à Vélo** (www.loireavelo.fr) maintains 800km of signposted routes from Cuffy (near Nevers) all the way to the Atlantic. Pick up a free guide from tourist offices, or download material (including route maps, audioguides and bike-hire details) from the website. Individual regions, like Anjou, Touraine, Centre or the Loiret (around Orléans), also have their own routes and accommodation guides. Tourist offices (and their websites) are well stocked with material.

If you'd like to cycle but want some help, **Bagafrance** (www.bagafrance.com) transports luggage and bikes, and many outfits rent electric bikes. Or consider a tour.

Détours de Loire (☑ 02 47 61 22 23; www.locationdevelos.com) Has bike-rental shops in Tours, Amboise, Blois and Saumur and myriad partners. Delivers bikes and also allows you to pick up and drop off bikes along the route for a small surcharge. Prices include a lock, helmet, repair kit and pump. Classic bikes cost €15/€60 per day/week, with extra days €5. Tandems cost €45/140 per day/week.

Les Châteaux à Vélo (☑ in Blois 02 54 78 62 52; www.chateauxavelo.com; per day €12-14) Bike-rental circuit between Blois, Chambord, Cheverny and Chaumont-sur-Loire; 400km of marked trails and minibus shuttle. Get route maps and MP3 guides from the website, or pick up brochures at local tourist offices.

Wheel Free (☑ 02 38 44 26 85; www.wheel-free.fr; 33 rue du Géneral de Gaulle, St-Jean le Blanc; 1st/additional days €20/9.60) Rents, delivers and picks up electric bikes.

- -

☞ Tours & Activities

Boat

The Loire offers few opportunities to get out on the water: the currents are often too unpredictable to navigate safely, but it's not completely off-limits. Check at tourist offices for boat excursions or kayak rentals. The Saumur/Candes-St-Martin area has many.

Specialised Tours

Tourist offices are stocked with info on local excursions by hot-air balloon or with a specialised theme, like cycling or wine tasting. Saumur is particularly rich in equestrian tours.

Cheval et Châteaux (www.cheval-et-chateaux.com; multiday tours per person €1114-2229) Experienced equestrian and guide Anne-France Launay leads four- to seven-day horseback excursions to some of the Loire's best-known châteaux, with overnights in castle-based B&Bs, including gourmet meals and wine.

Art Montgolfières (☑ 02 54 32 08 11; www.art-montgolfieres.fr; 1/2 persons €205/390) Perfect if you've ever dreamed of soaring over a château in a hot-air balloon! Spend one hour aloft and then quaff a celebratory glass of bubbly (or two).

Château du Petit Thouars Wine & Boat Excursion (☑ 02 47 95 96 40; www.chateaudptwines.com; St-Germain-sur-Vienne;

B&Bs, camping and vacation rentals: www.gites-de-france-loiret.com, www.gites-de-france-blois.com
Cycling routes: www.loireavelo.fr
Loire Valley châteaux: www.leschateauxdelaloire.org
Loire Valley heritage site: www.valdeloire.fr
Regional transport details: www.destineo.fr
Wines of the Loire: www.vinsvaldeloire.fr

adult/child €30/15) Sail on a handmade wooden boat for two hours from a vineyard to nearby villages like Montsoreau or Chinon, while tasting the vintner's wines with local snacks.

ORLÉANAIS

Taking its name from the historic city of Orléans, famous for its Joan of Arc connections, the Orléanais is the northern gateway to the Loire Valley. In the east are the ecclesiastical treasures of St-Benoît-sur-Loire and Germigny-des-Prés, while to the south lies the marshy Sologne, historically a favourite hunting ground for France's kings and princes.

Orléans

POP 117,988

There's a definite big-city buzz around the broad boulevards, flashy boutiques and elegant buildings of Orléans, 100km south of Paris. It's a city with enduring heritage: an important settlement by the time of the Romans' arrival, Orléans sealed its place in history in 1429 when a young peasant girl by the name of Jeanne d'Arc (Joan of Arc) rallied the armies of Charles VII and staged a spectacular rout against the besieging English forces, a key turning point in the Hundred Years War. Six centuries later, the Maid of Orléans still exerts a powerful hold on the French imagination, and you'll discover statues and museums dedicated to her around town. The city's charming, mostly pedestrianised medieval quarter stretches from the River Loire north to rue Jeanne d'Arc, and has an outstanding art museum and fantastical cathedral.

Orléans

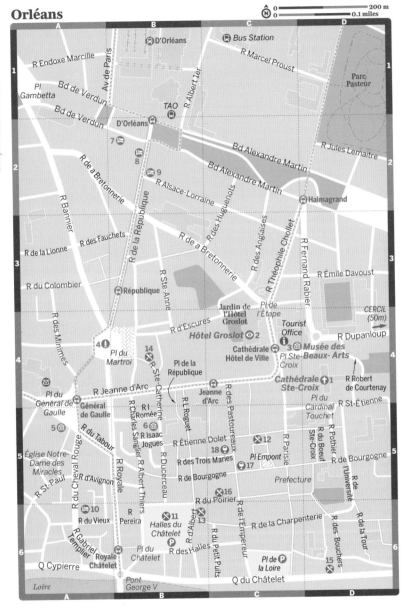

0 ———— 200 m
0 ———— 0.1 miles

Parc Pasteur

Bus Station

R Marcel Proust

R Endoxe Marcille

Pl Gambetta

Bd de Verdun

Bd de Verdun

Av de Paris

R Albert 1er

D'Orléans

TAO

D'Orléans

R Jules Lemaître

R de la Bretonnerie

R Alsace-Lorraine

Bd Alexandre Martin

Bd Alexandre Martin

Halmagrand

R Banner

R des Fauchets

R de la République

R de a Bretonnerie

R des Huguenots

R des Anglaises

R Théophile Chollet

R Fernand Rabier

R de la Lionne

R du Colombier

République

R Ste-Anne

R Émile Davoust

R des Minimes

Jardin de l'Hôtel Groslot

Pl de l'Étape

Tourist Office

CERCIL (50m)

R Dupanloup

R d'Escures

Hôtel Groslot

Cathédrale Hôtel de Ville

Musée des Beaux- Arts

Pl du Martroi

Pl Ste-Croix

Cathédrale Ste-Croix

R Robert de Courtenay

Pl du Général de Gaulle

R Jeanne d'Arc

Ste-Catherine

Jeanne d'Arc

R des Pastoureaux

Pl du Cardinal Touchet

R St-Étienne

Général de Gaulle

Pl de la République

R Charles Sanglier

R L Roquet

R Romée

R Isaac Jogues

R Étienne Dolet

R Parisie

R du Bœuf Ste-Croix

R Pothier

R de Bourgogne

Église Notre-Dame des Miracles

R du Tabour

R Albert Thiers

R Ducerceau

R des Trois Maries

R de Bourgogne

Pl Empont

Prefecture

R de l'Université

R St-Paul

R Cheval Rouge

R Royale

R d'Avignon

R du Vieux

R Pereira

Halles du Châtelet

R du Poirier

R d'Albert

R de l'Empereur

R de la Charpenterie

R des Bouchers

R de la Tour

R Gabriel Templier

Royale Châtelet

Pl du Châtelet

R des Halles

R du Petit Puits

Pl de la Loire

Q Cypierre

Loire

Pont George V

Q du Châtelet

◉ Sights & Activities

The tourist office runs guided **walking tours** (€6.50; generally in French, but occasionally English; reserve ahead) of Orléans. Some are combined with a riverboat cruise. The office also sells the self-guided walking tour brochure *9 Balades Entre Ciel et Loire* (€0.50).

★ Cathédrale Ste-Croix
Cathedral

(www.orleans.catholique.fr/cathedrale; place Ste-Croix; ◷ 9.15am-noon & 2.15-5.45pm) In a country

Orléans

⊙ Top Sights

1	Cathédrale Ste-Croix	D4
2	Hôtel Groslot	C4
3	Musée des Beaux-Arts	C4

⊙ Sights

4	Joan of Arc Statue	A4
5	Maison de Jeanne d'Arc	A5
6	Musée Historique et Archéologique	B5
	Place du Martroi	(see 4)

🛏 Sleeping

7	Hôtel Archange	B2
8	Hôtel d'Arc	B2
9	Hôtel de l'Abeille	B2
10	Hôtel Marguerite	A6

⊗ Eating

11	Covered Market	B6
12	La Dariole	C5
13	La Parenthèse	B6
14	Le Brin de Zinc	B4
15	Le Lièvre Gourmand	D6
16	Les Fagots	C5

⊙ Drinking & Nightlife

17	McEwan's	C5
18	Ver di Vin	C5

of jaw-dropping churches, the Cathédrale Ste-Croix still raises a gasp. Towering above place Ste-Croix, Orléans' Flamboyant Gothic cathedral was originally built in the 13th century and then underwent collective tinkering by successive monarchs. Joan of Arc came and prayed here on 8 May 1429, and was greeted with a procession of thanks for saving the town. It was Henri IV who kicked off the cathedral's reconstruction in 1601. Louis XIII (r 1610–43) restored the choir and nave, Louis XIV (r 1643–1715) was responsible for the transept, and Louis XV (r 1715–74) and Louis XVI (r 1774–92) rebuilt the western facade, including its huge arches and wedding-cake towers. Inside, slender columns soar skywards towards the vaulted ceiling and 106m spire, completed in 1895, while a series of vividly coloured stained-glass windows relates the life of St Joan, who was canonised in 1920.

★ **Musée des Beaux-Arts**   Art Museum

(☑ 02 38 79 21 55; www.orleans.fr; 1 rue Fernand Rabier; adult/child incl audioguide €4/free, 1st Sun of the month free; ⊙ 10am-6pm Tue-Sun) Orléans' five-storeyed fine-arts museum is a treat, with an excellent selection of Italian, Flemish and Dutch paintings (including works by Correggio, Velázquez and Bruegel), as well as a huge collection by French artists such as Léon Cogniet (1794–1880) and Orléans-born Alexandre Antigna (1817–78), and Paul Gauguin (1848–1903), who spent some of his youth in Orléans. Among the treasures are a rare set of 18th-century pastels by Maurice Quentin de la Tour and Jean-Baptiste Chardin.

A ticket to the Musée des Beaux-Arts also grants entry to the Musée Historique et Archéologique.

★ **Hôtel Groslot**   Historic Mansion

(place de l'Étape; ⊙ 10am-noon & 2-6pm Sun-Fri, 5-7pm Sat) **FREE** The Renaissance Hôtel Groslot was built in the 15th century as a private mansion for Jacques Groslot, a city bailiff, and later used as Orléans' town hall during the Revolution. The neomedieval interior, with some original furnishings, is extravagant, especially the ornate bedroom in which 16-year-old King François II died in 1560 (now used for marriages). The rear gardens are lovely.

Maison de Jeanne d'Arc   Museum

(☑ 02 38 68 32 63; www.jeannedarc.com.fr; 3 place du Général de Gaulle; adult/child €4/free; ⊙ 10am-6pm Tue-Sun Apr-Sep, 2-6pm Tue-Sun Oct-Mar) The best place to get an overview of Joan of Arc's life story is this reconstruction of the 15th-century house that hosted her in 1429 (the original was destroyed by British bombing in 1940). Start with its main feature: a 15-minute movie (in French or English) tracing her origins and historical impact. Upstairs are the archives of the world's largest Joan of Arc research centre.

Musée Historique et Archéologique   Archaeology Museum

(☑ 02 38 79 25 60; 21 rue Ste-Catherine; admission incl in ticket to Musée des Beaux-Arts; ⊙ 1.30-5.45pm Tue-Fri, 9.30am-noon & 1.30-5.45pm Sat, 2-6pm Sun) The centrepiece of the museum in the Renaissance mansion is the Salle Jeanne d'Arc, filled with artistic representations of the Maid of Orléans, from a late 15th-century Swiss tapestry and fine paintings to 20th-century mustard jars. The museum's Gallo-Roman collection includes several rare bronzes recovered from the Loire.

LOIRE VALLEY FOR KIDS

» Be razzle-dazzled by magic and illusion at Maison de la Magie (p63) in Blois.

» Prowl through ancient cave dwellings near Saumur and Doué-la-Fontaine (p84).

» Celebrate comic book character Tintin with cracks of lightning and pounding thunder at Château de Cheverny (p66).

» Play in the parks around pointy Pagode de Chanteloup (p72) at Amboise.

» Book ahead for amazing horse acrobatics at Saumur's semi-monthly Cadre Noir public presentations (p79).

Place du Martroi Square

Three of Orléans' main boulevards (rue Bannier, rue de la République and rue Royale) converge on place du Martroi, where you'll find a huge bronze **statue** (1855) by Denis Foyatier, depicting St Joan atop a prancing steed. A Friday evening vegetable and flea **market** (5pm to 10pm) sets up here.

CERCIL Museum

(Musée-Mémorial des Enfants du Vel d'Hiv; ☑ 02 38 42 03 91; www.cercil.fr; 45 rue du Bourdon-Blanc; adult/child €3/free; ☉ 2-6pm Tue-Fri & Sun) Moving exhibits (in French) document the deportation of the Jews – especially the children of the area – during WWII, and include a shack from one of the region's three internment camps (Beaune-la-Rolande, Pithiviers and Jargeau). Find it one block northeast of the cathedral.

✿✿ Festivals & Events

Fêtes de Jeanne d'Arc Cultural Festival

(www.fetesjeannedarc.com) Since 1430 the Orléanais have celebrated the Fêtes de Jeanne d'Arc in late April and early May, commemorating the liberation of Orléans from the English. A week of street parties, enormous medieval costume parades and concerts ends with a procession and morning Mass at the cathedral on 8 May.

🛏 Sleeping

Hôtel Archange Boutique Hotel €

(☑ 02 38 54 42 42; www.hotelarchange.com; 1 bd de Verdun; r €55-90, q €90-135; ☎) Gilded mirrors, cherub murals and sofas shaped like giant hands greet you at this station hotel. Splashy colour schemes spice up rooms, and shuttered windows combat daytime tram noise.

★ **Hôtel de l'Abeille** Historic Hotel €€

(☑ 02 38 53 54 87; www.hoteldelabeille.com; 64 rue Alsace-Lorraine; d €98-135, q €170-195; ☎) Bees buzz, floorboards creak and vintage Orléans posters adorn the walls at this gorgeous turn-of-the-century house, run by the same family for four generations. It's deliciously old-fashioned, from the scuffed pine floors and wildly floral wallpapers to the hefty dressers and bee-print curtains. For breakfast (€12) there's a choice of coffees, teas, juices and exotic jams. Only downside: no lift.

Hôtel d'Arc Hotel €€

(☑ 02 38 53 10 94; www.hoteldarc.fr; 37ter rue de la République; s €112-190, d €126-230; ✳@☎) Ride the vintage-style lift to 35 slick rooms at this Best Western–affiliated hotel, conveniently located between the train station and the pedestrianised centre. Rooms vary in size but all are done up comfortably. The Prestige and Deluxe rooms come with plush robes.

Hôtel Marguerite Hotel €€

(☑ 02 38 53 74 32; www.hotel-marguerite.fr; 14 place du Vieux Marché; d €70-145, q €120-145; ☎) This basic but solid hotel wins points for its friendly reception and central location. Opt for a superior room if you like your bathroom sparkling and your shower powerful; some of these rooms were recently renovated. Free bike parking.

✕ Eating

Orléans is a great food city. Reserve ahead at top restaurants.

Les Fagots Traditional French €

(☑ 02 38 62 22 79; 32 rue du Poirier; menus €13-17; ☉ noon-2pm & 7.30-10pm Tue-Sat) Delightful smoky smells lure you into this unpretentious eatery whose menu revolves around roasted meat. The Auvergnat owner cooks everything over an open fire, including grilled tomatoes and baked potatoes slathered with crème fraiche and chives.

★ La Parenthèse
Modern French €€

(☑ 02 38 62 07 50; www.restaurant-la-parenthese. com; 26 place du Châtelet; menus lunch €15-17, dinner €24-28; ☺ lunch & dinner Tue-Sat) Book ahead for this very popular restaurant, a labour of love for youthful chef David Sterne. Produce from the Halles marketplace across the street forms the basis for ever-changing, bargain-priced *plats du jour* (€10), plus creative lunch and dinner menus. Choose from relaxed sidewalk seating or two more refined indoor dining rooms.

La Dariole
Regional Cuisine €€

(☑ 02 38 77 26 67; 25 rue Étienne Dolet; menus €21-26; ☺ noon-1.30pm Mon-Fri, 7.30-10pm Tue & Fri) One of Orléans' smartest, most popular restaurants, La Dariole specialises in regional food. Inventive starters such as gazpacho with an asparagus-avocado charlotte are followed by mains like wine-braised beef with artichokes, and desserts like vanilla bean crème brûlée with fresh raspberries.

Le Brin de Zinc
Bistro €€

(☑ 02 38 53 38 77; www.groupedegenne.com; 62 rue Ste-Catherine; menus lunch €16, dinner €22-27; ☺ 11.45am-2.30pm & 6.45-10.30pm daily, to 11pm Fri & Sat) Battered signs, old telephones and a vintage scooter decorate this old-world-style bistro serving French classics till late. On summer evenings, the sunny sidewalk tables are a big draw, as are daily specials – mussels, *frites* (chips) and a beer for €12, anyone?

★ Le Lièvre Gourmand
Gastronomic €€€

(☑ 02 38 53 66 14; www.lelievregourmand.com; 28 quai du Châtelet; menus lunch €35, dinner from €45; ☺ noon-1.15pm & 8-9.30pm Wed-Mon) From the moment you settle into one of the comfy couches in this beautiful townhouse overlooking the Loire, the relaxed, lovely pampering begins. You'll get a perfect *amuse-bouche* (small bite) with your aperitif as you decide on a set of courses...each a creative duo of preparations: hot and cold. Think delicate foams and infusions in unexpected combinations with seasonal ingredients, like new asparagus in spring.

Self-Catering

Covered Market
Food Market

(place du Châtelet; ☺ 8.30am-7pm Tue-Sat, to 12.30pm Sun) Inside the Halles du Châtelet shopping centre.

🍷 Drinking & Nightlife

The free *Orléans Poche* (www.orleanspoche. com, in French) details cultural happenings. Rue de Bourgogne and rue du Poirier are chock-a-block with drinking holes.

Ver di Vin
Wine Bar

(☑ 02 38 54 47 42; www.verdivin.com; 2 rue des Trois Maries; ☺ 6pm-1am Tue-Sat; ☎) This popular subterranean wine bar is run by experienced sommeliers; reserve ahead for occasional *dégustation* (tasting) nights.

McEwan's
Pub

(250 rue de Bourgogne; ☺ 4pm-1am Mon-Sat) Scottish-themed pub popular for its wide variety of whiskies and beers on tap, and regular rugby and football broadcasts.

ℹ Information

Tourist Office (☑ 02 38 24 05 05; www. tourisme-orleans.com; 2 place de l'Étape; ☺ 9.30am-1pm & 2-6.30pm Mon-Sat May-Jun & Sep, 9am-7pm Mon-Sat, 10am-1pm & 2-5pm Sun Jul & Aug, shorter hours rest of year) Wellstocked with guides (like the Loiret cycle guide) and event information, in many languages.

BLÉSOIS

The countryside around the former royal seat of Blois is surrounded by some of the country's finest châteaux, including graceful Cheverny, little-visited Beauregard and the turret-topped supertanker château to end them all, Chambord.

Blois
POP 48,393

Looming on a rocky outcrop on the northern bank of the Loire, Blois' historic château (formerly the feudal seat of the powerful counts of Blois) provides a whistle-stop tour through the key periods of French history and architecture. Blois suffered heavy bombardment during WWII, and the modern-day town is mostly the result of postwar reconstruction, but a small area of twisting medieval streets remain.

◉ Sights

Blois château, *son et lumière* show and/or Maison de la Magie combination tickets save some cash. Admission to any two attractions costs €15/7 per adult/child or for all three €19.50/10.50. Kids under six are free.

★ **Château Royal de Blois** Château

(☑ 02 54 90 33 33; www.chateaudeblois.fr; place du Château; adult/child €10/5, audioguide €4, English tours Jul & Aug free; ◷ 9am-6pm Apr-Jun, Oct & Nov, to 7pm Jul & Aug, shorter hours rest of year) Intended more as an architectural showpiece than a military stronghold, Blois' château bears the creative mark of several successive French kings. It makes an excellent introduction to the châteaux of the Loire Valley, with elements of Gothic (13th century), Flamboyant Gothic (1498–1503), early Renaissance (1515–24) and classical (1630s) architecture in its four grand wings.

The most famous feature of the Renaissance wing, the royal apartments of François I and Queen Claude, is the loggia staircase, decorated with salamanders and curly Fs (heraldic symbols of François I).

Highlights also include the bedchamber in which Catherine de Médici (Henri II's machi-avellian wife) died in 1589. According to Alexandre Dumas, the queen stashed her poisons in secret cupboards behind the elaborately panelled walls of the studiolo, one of the few rooms in the castle with its original decor.

The 2nd-floor king's apartments were the setting for one of the bloodiest episodes in the château's history: in 1588 Henri III had his arch-rival, Duke Henri I de Guise, murdered by royal bodyguards (the king hid behind a tapestry). He had the duke's brother, the Cardinal de Guise, killed the next day. Henri III himself was murdered just eight months later by a vengeful monk. Period paintings chronicle the gruesome events.

In spring and summer, don't miss the nightly son et lumière (Sound & Light Show; ☑ 02 54 55 26 31; adult/child €8/5; ◷ 10pm Apr, May & Sep, 10.30pm Jun-Aug), which brings the château's history and architecture to life with dramatic lighting and narration.

WINE IN THE LOIRE VALLEY

Splendid scenery and densely packed vineyards make the Loire Valley a classic wine touring destination, with a range of excellent red, white and crémant (sparkling wines). Armed with the free map from the wine association (www.vinsvaldeloire.fr, with a US representative at www.loirevalleywine.com) called *Sur la Route des Vins de Loire* (On the Loire Wine Route) or the *Loire Valley Vineyards* booklet, available online, at area tourist offices and *maisons de vins* (literally, wine houses), you can put together a never-ending web of wine-tasting itineraries, drawing from over 320 'open cellars'. The *maisons des vins* in Blois, Tours, Cheverny, Saumur and Angers offer tasting and guidance on Loire wines, and have loads of information.

Anjou and Saumur alone have 30 AOCs (Appellation d'Origine Contrôlée), and Touraine has nine, including some lively gamays, a fruity, light-bodied wine. The Val de Loire (www.vinsvaldeloire.fr) website has a complete primer.

The most predominant red is cabernet franc, though you'll also find cabernet sauvignon, pinot noir and others. Appellations include Anjou, Saumur-Champigny, Bourgueil and Chinon.

For whites, Vouvray's chenin blancs are excellent, and Sancerre and the appellation across the river, Pouilly-Fumé, produce great sauvignon blancs. Cour-Cheverny is made from the lesser known Romorantin grape. Savennières, near Angers, has both a dry and a sweet chenin blanc.

The bubbly appellation Crémant de Loire spans many communities, but you can easily find it around Montrichard (eg Château Monmousseau), and other bubblies include Saumur Brut and Vouvray.

One of the most densely packed stretches for wine tasting along the River Loire itself is around Saumur. Towns with multiple tasting rooms (from west to east) include St-Hilaire-St-Florent (where you'll find Ackerman, Langlois-Château and Veuve Amiot), Souzay Champigny (home to Château Villeneuve and Clos des Cordeliers) and Parnay (Château de Parnay and Château de Targé).

Just east of Tours, another hot spot includes Rochecorbon (home to Blanc Foussy), Vouvray (Domaine Huet l'Echansonne, Château Moncontour and several others) and Montlouis-sur-Loire. You'll find a Cave des Producteurs representing multiple producers in the latter two towns. Designate a driver (or hop on your bike), grab your map and explore!

⭐ Maison de la Magie   Museum

(www.maisondelamagie.fr; 1 place du Château; adult/child €9/5; ⊙10am-12.30pm & 2-6.30pm Apr-Aug, 2-6.30pm Mon-Fri, 10am-12.30pm & 2-6.30pm Sat & Sun Sep) Opposite the château you can't miss the former home of watchmaker, inventor and conjurer Jean Eugène Robert-Houdin (1805–71), whose name was later adopted by American magician Harry Houdini. Dragons emerge roaring from the windows on the hour, while the museum inside hosts daily magic shows, exhibits on the history of magic, displays of optical trickery and a short historical film about Houdini.

Old City   Historic Quarter

Despite serious damage by German attacks in 1940, Blois' old city is worth exploring, especially around 17th-century Cathédrale St-Louis (place St-Louis; ⊙9am-6pm), with its lovely multistoreyed bell tower, dramatically floodlit after dark. Most of the stained glass inside was installed by Dutch artist Jan Dibberts in 2000.

Across the square, the facade of Maison des Acrobates (3bis place St-Louis) – one of the few 15th-century houses to survive – is decorated with wooden sculptures of medieval farces. Another example around the corner at No 13 rue Pierre de Blois is called Hôtel de Villebrême.

Lovely panoramas unfold across town from the peaceful Jardins de l'Évêché and the top of the Escalier Denis Papin.

Fondation du Doute   Art Museum

(www.fondationdudoute.fr; 6 rue Franciade; adult/child €7/3, joint tickets available with château & Maison de la Magie; ⊙2-6.30pm Tue-Sun Jun-Aug, shorter hours rest of year) This slick contemporary art museum, opened in 2013, includes rotating exhibitions of emerging and international artists, and a cafe.

- - - - - - - - - - - - - - - - - -

☞ Tours

The tourist office offers walking tour brochures (€2) and guided French-language tours. Château guides run 1½-hour French-language city tours (€5/3 per adult/child). There's an English-language tour on Friday in July and August.

Carriage Rides   Carriage Ride

(📞02 54 87 57 62; www.attelagesdeblois.com; adult/child €7/4; ⊙2-6pm Apr-Jun & Sep, 11am-7pm Jul & Aug) Horse-drawn carriages clop around town from the château's main gate.

Observatoire Loire   Boat Trips

(📞02 54 56 09 24; www.observatoireloire.fr; 4 rue Vauvert; adult/child €9.50/7; ⊙May-Sep) Sets out from the Blois quayside aboard a traditional *futreau* (flat-bottomed barge).

- - - - - - - - - - - - - - - - - -

🛏 Sleeping

⭐ Côté Loire   Hotel €

(📞02 54 78 07 86; www.coteloire.com; 2 place de la Grève; r €59-95; 🖧) Spotless rooms come in cheery checks, bright pastels and the odd bit of exposed brick; some have Loire views. Breakfast (€10.50) is served on a quaint interior wooden deck, and the restaurant (*menus* €21 to €31) dishes up delicious local cuisine. Find it a block off the river, southwest of Pont Jaques Gabriel.

Hôtel Anne de Bretagne   Hotel €

(📞02 54 78 05 38; www.hotelannedebretagne.com; 31 av du Dr Jean Laigret; s €47, d €56-60, q €85; 🖧) This creeper-covered hotel three blocks east of the train station has friendly staff and a bar full of polished wood and vintage pictures. Brightly coloured rooms have flowery wallpaper and bold bedspreads.

Le Monarque   Hotel €

(📞02 54 78 02 35; www.hotel-lemonarque.com; 61 rue Porte Chartraine; s €47, d €60-67, q €85-87; ❄🖧) Modern and no-nonsense, this hotel sits at the edge of the old city, and offers comfort, cleanliness and a restaurant.

RV Parking   Campground €

(📞02 54 70 58 30) Contact the tourist office about its RV parking: one near the castle has power, waste disposal and showers (€5).

Les Salamandres   B&B €

(📞02 54 20 69 55; www.salamandres.fr; 1 rue de St-Dyé, Montlivault; r incl breakfast €59-75) To get off the beaten path, head to the quaint village of Montlivault, 12km northeast of Blois, on the southern bank of the Loire, and shack up in a family-owned, cheery *chambre d'hôte* (B&B) just a hop, skip and jump from Chambord. In an 18th-century wine estate, Martine and Jean-Claude offer simple, homey rooms and loads of regional knowledge. You'll need your own wheels to get there, though.

⭐ La Maison de Thomas   B&B €€

(📞02 54 46 12 10; www.lamaisondethomas.fr; 12 rue Beauvoir; r incl breakfast €90; 🖧) Four spacious rooms and a friendly welcome await

Château de Chambord

travelers at this beautiful B&B on a pedestrianised street halfway between the château and the cathedral. There's bike storage in the interior courtyard and a wine cellar where you can sample local vintages.

✗ Eating

Le Coup de Fourchette
Bistro €

(☑ 02 54 55 00 24; 15 Quai de la Saussaye; lunch/dinner menus €12/17; ⊗ noon-2pm Mon-Sat, 7-10pm Thu-Sat) Simple, delectable regional cuisine is dished up with a smile in this mod eatery with a few outdoor tables. Popular with locals, it offers some of Blois' best cheaper eats.

Les Planches
Italian €

(☑ 02 54 55 08 00; 5 rue Grenier à Sel; mains €10-16; ⊗ noon-2pm & 7-10pm Mon-Sat) Tucked back in the old centre, on a sweet square with other nearby eating options, Les Planches is a Blois favourite for its wood-fired bruschetta, in the ground floor of a restored townhouse or out on the terrace.

Les Banquettes Rouges
French €€

(☑ 02 54 78 74 92; www.lesbanquettesrouges.com; 16 rue des Trois Marands; menus €17.50-32.50; ⊗ noon-2pm & 7-10pm Tue-Sat) Handwritten slate menus and wholesome food distinguish the 'Red Benches': pork with chorizo and rosemary, duck with lentils, and *fondant au chocolat* to top it off.

Au Bouchon Lyonnais
Bouchon €€

(☑ 02 54 74 12 87; www.aubouchonlyonnais.com; 25 rue des Violettes; lunch/dinner menus €16/23; ⊗ noon-1.45pm & 7-9.30pm Tue-Sat) The food at this classic neighbourhood bistro is out of a Lyonnais cookbook: *andouillette* (sausage made from pigs' intestines), quenelles (pike dumplings), snails and *salade lyonnaise* (green salad with croutons, egg and bacon bits).

L'Orangerie
Gastronomic €€€

(☑ 02 54 78 05 36; www.orangerie-du-chateau.fr; 1 av du Dr Jean Laigret; menus €35-80; ⊗ noon-1.30pm & 7-9pm Tue-Sat) This acclaimed eatery is cloud nine for connoisseurs of haute cuisine. Plates are artfully stacked (duck liver, langoustine, foie gras) and the sparkling salon would make Louis XIV envious. On summer nights, dine in the courtyard.

Self-Catering

Food Market
Food Market

(place Louis XII; ⊗ 8am-1pm Tue, Thu & Sat) Blois' thrice-weekly market.

☐ Drinking & Nightlife

The best bars are in the old town, particularly on place Ave Maria and in the small alleys off rue Foulerie.

ℹ️ Information

Tourist Office (📞 02 54 90 41 41; www.blois chambord.com; 23 place du Château; ⏱ 9am-7pm Apr-Sep, to 5pm Oct-Mar) Helpful, and sells joint châteaux tickets. Download the Visit' Blois smartphone app.

Château de Chambord

For full-blown château splendour, you can't top Château de Chambord (📞 information 02 54 50 40 00, tour & spectacle reservations 02 54 50 50 40; www.chambord.org; adult/child €11/9, parking €4; ⏱ 9am-6pm Apr-Sep, 10am-5pm Oct-Mar), one of the crowning examples of French Renaissance architecture, and by far the largest, grandest and most visited château in the Loire Valley. Begun in 1519 as a weekend hunting lodge by François I, it quickly snowballed into one of the most ambitious (and expensive) architectural projects ever attempted by any French monarch. This cityscape of turrets, chimneys and lanterns crowns some 440 rooms, 365 fireplaces and 84 staircases, including a famous double-helix staircase, reputedly designed by the king's chum, Leonardo da Vinci.

Construction was repeatedly halted by financial problems, design setbacks and military commitments (not to mention the kidnapping of the king's two sons in Spain), and, ironically, when Chambord was finally finished 30-odd years later François found his elaborate palace too draughty, preferring the royal apartments in Amboise and Blois. He only stayed here for 42 days during his entire reign from 1515 to 1547.

Despite its apparent complexity, Chambord is laid out according to simple mathematical rules. Each section is arranged on a system of symmetrical grid squares around a Maltese cross. At the centre stands the rectangular keep, crossed by four great hallways, and at each corner stands one of the castle's four circular bastions. Through the centre of the keep winds the famous staircase, with two intertwining flights of stairs leading up to the great lantern tower and the castle's rooftop, from where you can gaze out across the landscaped grounds and marvel at the Tolkienesque jumble of cupolas, domes, chimneys and lightning rods.

The most interesting rooms are on the 1st floor, including the king's and queen's chambers (complete with interconnecting passages to enable late-night hijinks) and a wing devoted to the thwarted attempts

of the Comte de Chambord to be crowned Henri V after the fall of the Second Empire. On the 2nd floor the eerie Museum of Hunting exhibits copious displays of weapons and hunting trophies. On the ground floor, an interesting multilanguage film relates the history of the castle's construction.

In a place of such ostentatious grandeur, it's often the smallest things that are most interesting: look out for the display of hundreds of cast-iron keys, one for each door in the château.

It's worth picking up the multilingual audio or video guide (audio adult/child version €5/2.50, video €6), if only to avoid getting lost around the endless rooms and corridors. Several times daily there are guided tours (adult/child 1hr tours €5/3, 2hr tours €7/5) in English, and during school holidays costumed tours entertain the kids. Outdoor spectacles held in summer include a daily equestrian show (www.ecuries-chambord.com; adult/child €11/8; ⏱ May-Sep).

Domaine National de Chambord

This huge hunting reserve (the largest in Europe) stretches for 54 sq km around the château, and is reserved solely for the use of high-ranking French government personalities (though somehow it's difficult to imagine

François Hollande astride a galloping stallion). About 10 sq km of the park is publicly accessible, with trails open to walkers, mountain bikers and horse riders.

Hire bikes at a rental kiosk (☑ 02 54 33 37 54; per hr/half-day €6/15; ☺ 10am-7pm Apr-Sep) near the *embarcadère* (jetty) on the River Cosson, where you can also rent boats. It's great for wildlife-spotting, especially in September and October during the deer mating season. Observation towers dot the park; set out at dawn or dusk to spot stags, boars and red deer.

Or, jump aboard a Land Rover Safari tour (☑ 02 54 50 50 40; adult/child €18/12; ☺ Apr-Sep) conducted by French-speaking guides with an intimate knowledge of where to see the best wildlife.

❶ Getting There & Away

Chambord is 16km east of Blois, 45km southwest of Orléans and 17km northeast of Cheverny. The TLC shuttle on the Blois–Chambord–Cheverny–Beauregard–Blois circuit costs €6, takes 40 minutes from Blois, and runs mid-April to August.

Château de Cheverny

Thought by many to be the most perfectly proportioned château of all, Château de Cheverny (☑ 02 54 79 96 29; www.chateau-cheverny.fr; adult/child €10/7; ☺ 9am-7pm Apr-Sep, 10am-5pm Oct-Mar) represents the zenith of French classical architecture: the perfect blend of symmetry, geometry and aesthetic order. Since its construction between 1625 and 1634 by Jacques Hurault, an intendant to Louis XII, the castle has hardly been altered, and its interior decoration includes some of the most sumptuous furnishings, tapestries and objets d'art anywhere in the Loire Valley.

Tintin fans might find the château's facade oddly familiar: Hergé used it as a model (minus the two end towers) for Moulinsart (Marlinspike) Hall, the ancestral home of Tintin's irascible sidekick, Captain Haddock. A dynamic exhibition, Les Secrets de Moulinsart (combined ticket with château adult/child €14/9.90), explores the Tintin connections with re-created scenes, thunder and other special effects.

The interior of Château de Cheverny was designed by Jean Monier, known for his work on Luxembourg Palace for Queen Marie de Médici. Highlights include a formal dining room with panels depicting the story of Don Quixote, the king's chamber with murals relating stories from Greek mythology, a bridal chamber and children's playroom (complete with Napoléon III–era toys). The guards' room is full of pikestaffs, claymores and suits of armour – including a tiny one fit for a kid.

The Hurault family has owned (and inhabited) the castle for the last six centuries and their fabulous art collection includes a portrait of Jeanne of Aragon by Raphael's studio, an 18th-century De la Tour pastel, and a who's who of court painters. Keep your eyes open for the certificate signed by US president George Washington. Behind the main château, the 18th-century orangerie (where many priceless artworks, including the Mona Lisa, were stashed during WWII) is now a tearoom.

Near the château's gateway, the kennels house pedigreed French pointer/English foxhound hunting dogs still used by the owners of Cheverny. Feeding time, known as the Soupe des Chiens, takes place daily at 5pm April to September and 3pm Monday, Wednesday, Thursday and Friday, October to March.

❶ Getting There & Away

Cheverny is on the D102, 16km southeast of Blois and 17km southwest of Chambord. Azalys' Blois shuttle is €2 and takes 30 minutes. The TLC shuttle on the Blois–Chambord–Cheverny–Beauregard–Blois circuit costs €6, takes one hour from Blois, and runs mid-April to August.

Château de Chaumont

Set on a defensible bluff with sweeping views along the Loire, Château de Chaumont-sur-Loire (☑ 02 54 20 99 22; www.domaine-chaumont.fr; adult/child €10.50/6.50, with gardens €16/11; ☺ 10am-6.30pm Apr-Sep, to 6pm Oct-Mar) presents an elegantly streamlined medieval face, with its cylindrical corner turrets and sturdy drawbridge, though its interior furnishings date almost exclusively from the 19th century. At least two earlier fortresses occupied the site (whose name derives from Chauve Mont, 'Bald Hill'), but the main construction for the present château began around 1465 under Pierre d'Amboise.

Visit Chaumont's elaborate gardens independently or with the château; they're at their finest during the annual Festival International des Jardins (International Garden Festival; adult/child €12/7.50; ☺ 10am-7pm late Apr-Oct).

Originally a strictly defensive fortress, Chaumont-sur-Loire became a short-lived residence for Catherine de Médici following the death of Henri II in 1560, and later passed into the hands of Diane de Poitiers (Henri II's mistress), who was forced by Catherine to swap the altogether grander surroundings of Chenonceau for Chaumont. Savvy Diane used Chaumont's vast landholdings, but there is no evidence she ever lived in the castle.

In the second half of the 18th century, its owner, Jacques-Donatien Le Ray, a supporter of the American Revolution and an intimate of Benjamin Franklin, had the decrepit north wing removed. In 1875, Princess de Broglie, heiress to the Say sugar fortune, bought the château and thoroughly renovated and furnished it. The most impressive room is the council chamber, with its original majolica-tiled floor, plundered from a palace in Palermo. Also, don't miss the écuries (stables), built in 1877 to house the Broglies' horses in sumptuous style. A fine collection of vintage carriages and equestrian gear is displayed inside.

It's worth getting the informative multimedia guide (€4) or downloading the app.

❶ Getting There & Away

Chaumont-sur-Loire is 17km southwest of Blois. Onzain, a 2.5km walk from Chaumont across the Loire, has trains to Blois (€3.60, 10 minutes, 13 daily) and Tours (€8.60, 30 minutes, 10 daily). An Azalys shuttle runs from Blois.

Château de Beauregard

Less visited than its sister châteaux, peaceful Château de Beauregard (☑ 02 54 70 41 65; www.beauregard-loire.com; Cellettes; adult/child €12.50/5; ☺ 10.30am-6.30pm Apr-Sep, 1.30-5pm Mon-Fri, from 10.30am Sat & Sun mid-Feb–Mar & Oct–mid-Nov) has charms all its own. Built as yet another hunting lodge by François I, the highlight is an amazing portrait gallery depicting 327 notables of European royalty, clergy and intelligentsia. Spot famous faces including Christopher Columbus, Sir Francis Drake, Cardinal Richelieu, Catherine de Médicis, Anne de Bretagne, Henry VIII of England and his doomed wife Anne Boleyn, and every French king since Philippe VI. The quiet, 40-hectare grounds encompass numerous gardens, including the Garden of Portraits with 12 colour variations.

TLC's line 18 château shuttle from Blois, 8km southeast, serves Beauregard.

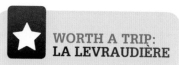

WORTH A TRIP: LA LEVRAUDIÈRE

Only 2km south of Château de Cheverny, amid 3 hectares of grassland, La Levraudière (☑ 02 54 79 81 99; www.lalevraudiere.fr; 1 chemin de la Levraudière; s/d/tr/q from €70/80/95/140) is a perfect blend of farm and modern style. In a peaceful, renovated 19th-century farmhouse, the B&B has a slab-like wooden table for breakfasts featuring fabulous homemade jams. But the crisp linens and meticulously kept house are the opposite of roughing it.

TOURAINE

Often dubbed the 'Garden of France', the Touraine region is famous for its rich food, tasty cheeses and notoriously pure French accent, as well as a smattering of glorious châteaux: some medieval (Langeais and Loches), others Renaissance (Azay-le-Rideau, Villandry and Chenonceau). The vibrant capital, Tours, offers loads of castle tours and transportation links.

Tours

POP 138,115

Bustling Tours has a zinging life of its own in addition to being one of the hubs of castle country. It's a smart, vivacious kind of place, with an impressive medieval centre, parks and a busy university of some 25,000 students. Hovering somewhere between the style of Paris and the conservative sturdiness of central France, Tours makes a useful staging post for exploring the Touraine.

◉ Sights & Activities

The old city encircles place Plumereau (locally known as place Plum), about 400m west of rue Nationale.

★ Musée des Beaux-Arts   Art Museum

(☑ 02 47 05 68 82; www.mba.tours.fr; 18 place François Sicard; adult/child €5/2.50, 1st Sun of the month free; ☺ 9am-12.45pm & 2-6pm Wed-Mon) This fine-arts museum in the archbishop's gorgeous 18th-century palace encircles free gardens and Gallo-Roman ruins, and flaunts grand rooms

Tours

N 0 ———— 200 m
0 ———— 0.1 miles

Rochecorbon (3.5km);
Amboise (23km)

St-Pierre-des-
Corps (5km)

R Dublineau

R Francois Clouet

R du Petit Pré

R du Rempart

**Cathédrale St-
Gatien** 2

Musée des
Beaux-Arts 3

Flower
Garden

R des Ursulines

R Jules Simon

Bd Heurteloup 17

Bd Heurteloup

R Édouard Vaillant

Gare de
Tours

5

Pl de la
Cathédrale 3

R Lavoisier

R Albert Thomas

Pl François
Sicard 9

R Bernard Palissy

Tourist
Office 9

Pl du
Général
Leclerc

Gare de
Tours

R de la Barre

Jardin
de la
Préfecture

R de Bordeaux

Av Charles Gille

R du Cygne

19

Pl Foire-
le-Roi

11

R Colbert 25

R Pimbert

R Corneille

R de la Préfecture

R de Buffon

Bus Station

Fil Vert

Fil Bleu

Pl de la
Préfecture

R Victor
Laloux

16

27

R Voltaire

R Berthelot

R de la Scellerie

R Émile Zola

R de la Préfecture

R Victor
Laloux

12

Pl Jean
Jaurès

**Musée du
Compagnonnage** 4

20

R Nationale

R Nationale

R Gambetta

Av de Grammont

Jean
Jaurès

Azay-le-Rideau (26km);
Loches (42km);
Chinon (46km)

Tours-Val de
Loire (12km)

R Nationale

R Étienne Pallu

No Public
Access

R du Commerce

23

Pl de la
Résistance

R des
Fusillés 15

R des Déportés

R Marceau

Bd Béranger

Bd Béranger

R de Constantine

R Néricault Destouches

R de Clocheville

R de la Grandière

R du Commerce

R de Jérusalem

**Basilique St-
Martin** 1

R des
Orfèvres

24

28

Pl
Plumereau

R de la Monnaie

R du
Châteauneuf

R Descartes

R Rapin

R Léonard
de Vinci

R Rabelais

R de la Paix

R Briçonnet

26

Pl du Grand
Marché 14

8 6

R des Halles

Pl Gaston
Paithou

R des Tanneurs

R du Mûrier

R Bretonneau

Pl du Grand
Marché

R Chanoineau

R de la Grandière

R Étienne Marcel

R Eugène Sue

10

21

R du Grand Marché

R des Balais

22

Les Halles

Jardin Botanique
(1km)

R du Petit St-Martin

R de la Grosse Tour

Pl des Halles

Pl de la
Victoire

R de la Victoire

R Georges
Delpérier

Tours

◉ Top Sights

1	Basilique St-Martin	B2
2	Cathédrale St-Gatien	F1
3	Musée des Beaux-Arts	F1
4	Musée du Compagnonnage	D1

◉ Sights

5	Cloître de la Psalette	F1
6	Musée St-Martin	B3
7	Tour Charlemagne	B2
8	Tour de l'Horloge	B2

⊕ Activities & Tours

9	Carriages	F2
10	Maison des Vins	A2

⊟ Sleeping

11	Hôtel Colbert	E1
12	Hôtel de l'Univers	E4
13	Hôtel des Arts	E2
14	Hôtel l'Adresse	B2
15	Hôtel Mondial	C1
16	Hôtel Ronsard	E1
17	Hôtel Val de Loire	G4

⊗ Eating

18	Barju	B2
19	Cap Sud	E1
20	L'Arôme	D1
21	L'Atelier Gourmand	A1
22	Le Zinc	A2
23	Tartines & Co	C1

◎ Drinking & Nightlife

24	L'Alexandra	B1
25	Pale	E1

✪ Entertainment

26	Excalibur	B1
27	Grand Théâtre	E2
28	Les Trois Orfèvres	B2

with works spanning several centuries. Highlights include paintings by Delacroix, Degas and Monet, a rare Rembrandt miniature and a Rubens *Madonna and Child.*

★ Cathédrale St-Gatien   Church

(place de la Cathédrale; ⊙ 9am-7pm) With its twin towers, flying buttresses, dazzling stained glass and gargoyles, this cathedral is a showstopper. The interior dates from the 13th to 16th centuries, and signs in English explain the intricate stained glass. The domed tops of the two 70m-high towers are Renaissance. On the north side is the Cloître de la

Psalette (adult/child €3/free; ⊙ 9.30am-12.30pm & 2-6pm Mon-Sat, 2-6pm Sun, closed Mon & Tue Oct-Mar), built from 1442 to 1524.

★ Musée du Compagnonnage   Museum

(☑ 02 47 21 62 20; www.museecompagnonnage. fr; 8 rue Nationale; adult/child €5.30/3.70; ⊙ 9am-12.30pm & 2-6pm, closed Tue mid-Sep–mid-Jun) France has long prided itself on its *compagnonnages,* guild organisations of skilled craftspeople who have been responsible for everything from medieval cathedrals to the Statue of Liberty. Dozens of professions – from pastry chefs to locksmiths – are celebrated here through impressive displays of their handiwork: exquisitely carved chests, handmade tools, booby-trapped locks, vintage barrels, outlandishly ornate cakes and more.

★ Basilique St-Martin   Church

(www.basiliquesaintmartin.fr; ⊙ 7.30am-7pm, to 9pm Jul & Aug) Tours was an important pilgrimage city thanks to soldier-turned-evangelist St Martin (c 317–97), bishop of Tours. In the 5th century a basilica was constructed above his tomb, and was later replaced by a 13th-century Romanesque one, but today only the Tour Charlemagne and Tour de l'Horloge (Clock Tower) remain. The current church was built in 1862 to house his relics, while the small Musée St-Martin (☑ 02 47 64 48 87; www.mba.tours.fr; 3 rue Rapin; adult/child €2/1; ⊙ 9.30am-1pm & 2-5pm Wed-Sun mid-Mar–mid-Nov) displays artefacts relating to the lost churches and the life of St Martin.

Jardin Botanique   Garden

(bd Tonnelle; ⊙ 7.45am-sunset) Tours' public parks include the 19th-century 5-hectare botanic garden with a tropical greenhouse, medicinal herb garden and petting zoo. Find it 1.6km west of place Jean Jaurès; bus 4 along bd Béranger stops nearby.

Maison des Vins   Wine Tasting

(☑ 02 47 60 55 21; www.vinsvaldeloire.fr; 25 rue du Grand Maré; ⊙ 10.30am-1pm & 3-7pm Tue-Sat) Get the lowdown on Loire vintages: tasting, sales, tours and tips.

- - - - - - - - - - - - - - - - - - -

☞ Tours

Tours is one of the major hubs for châteaux tours. The tourist office has a self-guided tour brochure, and leads guided walks (€6 to €9) in French. They recommend a free app through www.monument-tracker.com.

Carriages
Carriage Ride

(☑02 47 66 70 70; www.filbleu.fr; rides €1.40; ⊙10am, 11am, 3pm, 4pm & 5pm Tue-Sat, 3pm, 4pm & 5pm Sun May-Sep) Fifty-minute rides from place François Sicard near the cathedral. Drivers sell tickets.

- - - - - - - - - - - - - - - - -

🛏 Sleeping

⭐ Hôtel Ronsard
Boutique Hotel €

(☑02 47 05 25 36; www.hotel-ronsard.com; 2 rue Pimbert; s €63-77, d €73-85; ❋ @ 🖢) Pass beyond the bland exterior at this centrally located modern hotel and find easy comfort and good value. Halls are lined with colourful photographs, while sleek, immaculate rooms incorporate muted tones of grey with sparkling white linens.

Hôtel Colbert
Hotel €

(☑02 47 66 61 56; www.tours-hotel-colbert.fr; 78 rue Colbert; s €42-57, d €60-68; 🖢) In the heart of Tours' pedestrianised restaurant row, this family-run hotel offers a welcoming haven. Light sleepers could opt for 'Calme' rooms facing the quieter inner courtyard (which also doubles as a pleasant spot to relax, or park bikes overnight).

Hôtel Mondial
Hotel €

(☑02 47 05 62 68; www.hotelmondialtours.com; 3 place de la Résistance; s €60-70, d €65-80; 🖢) Overlooking place de la Résistance, this hotel boasts a fantastic city-centre position, with modernised, metropolitan rooms in funky greys, browns and scarlets. Reception is on the 2nd floor; no lift.

Hôtel Val de Loire
Hotel €

(☑02 47 05 37 86; www.hotelvaldeloire.fr; 33 bd Heurteloup; s with/without bathroom from €52/40, d with/without bathroom from €78/45; 🖢) Friendly management and bright rooms blending antiques and modern touches make this an excellent train station choice. Nicer back rooms downstairs have high ceilings and garden views, while less expensive top-floor rooms are tucked under eaves.

Hôtel des Arts
Hotel €

(☑02 47 05 05 00; www.hoteldesartstours.com; 40 rue de la Préfecture; s €35-49, d €40-54; 🖢) A sweet place, with charming management, Hôtel des Arts has tiny but fastidious, cheery rooms in oranges and siennas. Get one with a balcony for extra light.

⭐ Hôtel l'Adresse
Boutique Hotel €€

(☑02 47 20 85 76; www.hotel-ladresse.com; 12 rue de la Rôtisserie; s €55, d €78-105; ❋ 🖢) Looking for Parisian style in provincial Tours? You're in luck. On a pedestrianised street in the old quarter lies a boutique find, with rooms finished in slates, creams and ochres, designer sinks and reclaimed rafters.

Hôtel de l'Univers
Hotel €€€

(☑02 47 05 37 12; www.oceaniahotels.com/hotel-lunivers-tours; 5 bd Heurteloup; d €200-245; ❋ @ 🖢) Everyone from Ernest Hemingway to Édith Piaf has bunked at the Universe over its 150-year history. Enjoy the frescoed lobby balcony and appropriately glitzy rooms. Online discounts.

- - - - - - - - - - - - - - - - -

🍴 Eating

Pedestrianised rue Colbert is a great place to peruse your options: from classic French to Asian and Middle Eastern. The area around place Plumereau is crammed with cheap eats, although quality varies.

⭐ Le Zinc
French €

(☑02 47 20 29 00; lezinc37@gmail.com; 27 place du Grand Marché; menus €20; ⊙noon-2pm Tue & Thu-Sat, 7.30-10pm Thu-Tue, to 11pm Fri & Sat) More concerned with market-fresh staples (sourced from the nearby Halles) than with Michelin-star cachet, this bistro impresses with its authentic, well-presented country classics (duck breast, beef fillet, river fish).

Tartines & Co
Cafe €

(☑02 47 20 50 60; www.tartinesandco.com; 6 rue des Fusillés; sandwiches €10-13; ⊙11.45am-3pm & 7.15-10pm Tue-Sat) This snazzy little cafe reinvents the traditional *croque* (toasted sandwich) amid jazz and friendly chatter. Choose your topping (chicken, roasted veg, beef carpaccio, foie gras with artichokes) on toasted artisanal bread.

⭐ Cap Sud
Bistro €€

(☑02 47 05 24 81; www.capsudrestaurant.fr; 88 rue Colbert; menus lunch €14-19, dinner €26; ⊙noon-1.30pm & 7.15-9.30pm Tue-Sat) The hot-rod red interior combines nicely with genial service and refined culinary creations made from the freshest ingredients. Expect stylishly presented dishes such as warm St-Maure cheese with a pistachio-herb crumble and baby vegetables, or mullet fillet with sweet peppers, squid risotto and a ginger-tomato emulsion. Reserve ahead.

★ L'Arôme
Modern French €€

(☑ 02 47 05 99 81; larome.tours@yahoo.fr; 26 rue Colbert; menus lunch €13, 3-course dinner €24-41; ⊙ noon-1.30pm & 7.30-9.30pm Tue-Sat) One of Tours' most popular new spots, L'Arôme fills with lucky locals (they've reserved ahead) who come for the vivacious modern ambience and creative dishes, smack in the centre of town. Great wine selection too.

L'Atelier Gourmand
Modern French €€

(☑ 02 47 38 59 87; www.lateliergourmand.fr; 37 rue Étienne Marcel; lunch/dinner menus €13/25; ⊙ noon-2pm Tue-Fri, 7.30-10.30pm Mon-Sat) The puce-and-silver colour scheme is straight out of a Bret Easton Ellis novel, and everything's delivered with a modern spin. Many dishes feature intriguing blends of the sweet and savory, like pastis-flambéed prawns with sweet pea and mint risotto.

Barju
Seafood €€€

(☑ 02 47 64 91 12; www.barju.fr; 15 rue de Change; menus lunch €20-25, dinner €55; ⊙ noon-1.30pm & 7.30-9.30pm Tue-Sat) Lunch can be a super deal, but dinner is a more formal affair at this restaurant – a high-end date spot. Served with a smile in bright, contemporary rooms, the standout is the 'picque-nique' tasting menu with its continuous series of imaginative (often seafood-based) creations.

Self-Catering

Les Halles
Food Market

(www.halles-de-tours.com; place Gaston Paithou; ⊙ 7am-7.30pm Mon-Sat, 8am-1pm Sun) Big daily covered market.

Drinking & Nightlife

Place Plumereau and surrounding streets are loaded with drinking dens, which get stuffed to bursting on hot summer nights.

Pale
Pub

(cnr rue Colbert & place Foire-le-Roi; ⊙ noon-2am Tue-Sat, to midnight Sun; ☎) This quintessential, lively Irish pub, with a plethora of beers on tap, spills out onto tables in a small park and along pedestrianised rue Colbert, day and night.

L'Alexandra
Bar

(106 rue du Commerce; ⊙ 3pm-2am; ☎) Popular bar crammed with students and late-night boozers.

Excalibur
Club

(☑ 02 47 64 76 78; www.facebook.com/excalibur. tours; 35 rue Briçonnet; ⊙ midnight-6am Tue-Sat) Hot-and-heavy club in a converted ecclesiastical building.

☆ Entertainment

Get the low-down from free monthly *Tours. infos* (www.tours.fr), available around town.

Les Trois Orfèvres
Live Music

(☑ 02 47 64 02 73; 3orfevres.com; 6 rue des Orfèvres; ⊙ midnight-6am Wed-Sat) Grungy nightspot in the heart of the medieval quarter, where DJs and bands lean towards alternative and indie, and students hang out in force.

Grand Théâtre
Performing Arts

(☑ 02 47 60 20 20; www.operadetours.fr; 34 rue de la Scellerie; ⊙ box office 10am-noon & 1-5.45pm Tue-Sat) Hosts operas, symphonies, chamber music and other concerts.

❶ Information

Police Station (☑ 02 47 33 80 69; 70-72 rue Marceau; ⊙ 24hr)

SOS Médecins (☑ 02 47 38 33 33) Phone advice for medical emergencies.

Tourist Office (☑ 02 47 70 37 37; www.tours-tourisme.fr; 78-82 rue Bernard Palissy; ⊙ 8.30am-7pm Mon-Sat, 10am-12.30pm & 2.30-5pm Sun Apr-Sep, shorter hours rest of year) Abundant info; slightly reduced châteaux tickets.

❶ Getting There & Away

AIR

Tours Val de Loire Airport (TUF; ☑ 02 47 49 37 00; www.tours.aeroport.fr) Tours Val de Loire Airport, about 5km northeast of town, is linked to London's Stansted, Dublin (Ireland), Marseille, Marrakesh (Morocco) and Porto (Portugal) by Ryanair, and to Southampton (England) by Flybe.

CAR & MOTORCYCLE

Tours' perplexing one-way streets make driving a headache: park your car. Use an **underground garage** (per 24hr €11) such as the one below Les Halles, for stays of more than two hours. Check opening hours for the garage you choose; many are reduced on Sunday.

Avis (☑ 02 47 20 53 27; central train station; ⊙ 8am-12.30pm & 1.30-6pm Mon-Fri, 9am-noon & 2-6pm Sat) Also has locations at St-Pierre-des-Corps TGV station and the airport.

Château de Chenonceau

Spanning the languid Cher River via a series of supremely graceful arches, the Château de Chenonceau (☑02 47 23 90 07; www.chenonceau.com; adult/child €11/8.50, with audioguide €17/13.50; ☺ from 9am or 9.30am year-round, closes 5pm to 8pm depending on month) is one of the most elegant and unusual in the Loire Valley. You can't help but be swept up in the magical architecture, the fascinating history of prominent female owners, the glorious setting and the formal gardens and landscaped parkland.

The château's interior is crammed with wonderful furniture and tapestries, stunning original tiled floors and a fabulous art collection including works by Tintoretto, Correggio, Rubens, Murillo, Van Dyck and Ribera. This architectural fantasy land is largely the work of several remarkable women (hence its alternative name, Le Château des Dames: 'Ladies' Château'). The initial phase of construction started in 1515 for Thomas Bohier, a court minister of King Charles VIII, although much of the work and design was actually overseen by his wife, Katherine Briçonnet.

The château's distinctive arches and one of the formal gardens were added by Diane de Poitiers, mistress of King Henri II. Following Henri's death, Diane was forced to exchange Chenonceau for the rather less grand château of Chaumont by the king's scheming widow, Catherine de Médici, who completed the construction and added the huge yew-tree labyrinth and the western rose garden. Louise of Lorraine's most interesting contribution was her mourning room, on the top floor, all in black, to which she retreated when her husband, Henri III, was assassinated.

Chenonceau had an 18th-century heyday under the aristocratic Madame Dupin, who made the château a centre of fashionable society and attracted guests including Voltaire and Rousseau. Legend also has it that it was she who single-handedly saved the château from destruction during the Revolution, thanks to her popularity with local villagers.

The pièce de résistance is the 60m-long window-lined Grande Gallerie spanning the Cher, scene of many a wild party hosted by Catherine de Médici or Madame Dupin. During WWII the Cher also marked the boundary between free and occupied France; local legend has it that the Grand Gallery was used as the escape route for many refugees fleeing the Nazi occupation.

The top floor of the gallery has a superb exhibition illustrating the château's history. Chenonceau's smartphone app gives general background only; the audioguide is better.

Skip the drab wax museum and instead visit the gardens: it seems as if there's one of every kind imaginable (maze, English, vegetable, playground, flower...). In July and August the illuminated grounds are open for the Promenade Nocturne (adult/child €6/free; ☺ 9.30-11.30pm).

Croisières Fluviales La Bélandre (☑02 47 23 98 64; www.labelandre.com; adult/child €9.50/6.50; ☺ Apr-Oct) offers 50-minute boat trips along the Cher River in summer, passing directly beneath the château's arches.

ⓘ Getting There & Away

The château is located 34km east of Tours, 10km southeast of Amboise and 40km southwest of Blois. From Chenonceaux, the town just outside the château grounds (spelled with an 'x', unlike the château!), 10 daily trains run to Tours (€6.50, 24 minutes). Touraine Fil Vert's bus line C (€2.20) also runs once daily from Chenonceaux to Amboise (25 minutes) and Tours.

Amboise

POP 13,375

The childhood home of Charles VIII and the final resting place of the great Leonardo da Vinci, elegant Amboise is gorgeously arrayed on the southern bank of the Loire and overlooked by its inspiring 15th-century château. With some seriously posh hotels and a wonderful weekend market, Amboise has become a very popular base for exploring nearby châteaux, and coach tours arrive en masse to visit da Vinci's Clos Lucé. Rue Nationale is packed with interesting boutiques.

◉ Sights

Go to sights early in the day to avoid crowds, and buy tickets in advance at the tourist office during high season.

★ Château Royal d'Amboise   Château

(☑02 47 57 52 23; www.chateau-amboise.com; place Michel Debré; adult/child €10/7; ☺ 9am-7pm Jul & Aug, to 6pm Apr-Oct, shorter hours Nov-Mar) Elegantly tiered on a rocky escarpment above town, this easily defendable castle presented a formidable prospect to would-be attackers – but saw little military action. It was more often a

Amboise

weekend getaway from the official royal seat at Blois. Charles VIII (r 1483–98), born and bred here, was responsible for the château's Italianate remodelling in 1492. Today just a few of the original 15th- and 16th-century structures survive, notably the Flamboyant Gothic wing and Chapelle St-Hubert, the final resting place of Leonardo da Vinci. They have thrilling views to the river, town and gardens. The château was the site of much historical intrigue, including the kidnapping of François II in March 1560.

At the time of research, cylindrical Tour Hurtault with its ingenious sloping spiral ramp for easy carriage access, was closed for restoration.

★ Le Clos Lucé   Historic Building

(☑ 02 47 57 00 73; www.vinci-closluce.com; 2 rue du Clos Lucé; adult/child €14/9.50, joint family tickets reduced; ☉ 9am-8pm Jul & Aug, 9am-7pm Feb-Jun & Sep-Oct, 9am-6pm Nov & Dec, 10am-6pm Jan; 🚸) Leonardo da Vinci took up residence at this grand manor house in 1516 on the invitation of François I. An admirer of the Italian Renaissance, François named da Vinci 'first painter, engineer and king's architect'. Already 64 by the time he arrived, da Vinci spent his time sketching, tinkering and dreaming up new contraptions, scale models of which are now displayed throughout the home and its expansive gardens.

Visitors tour rooms where da Vinci worked and the bedroom where he drew his last breath on 2 May 1519. There is a free smartphone app, and a daily tour in English, Monday through Friday in July and August.

☞ Tours

Contact the tourist office about their slate of village, château and Clos Lucé walking tours in July and August.

Freemove Segway Tours   Segway Tour

(☑ 02 47 30 95 35; www.freemove.fr; 45/90min tours €27/47; ☉ 9.30am-1pm & 3-6.30pm May-Sep) This reservation-only Segway tour outfit also has tours in Blois, Loches and Tours.

⊨ Sleeping

Amboise has some of the smartest places to stay in the Loire Valley, but you'll need deep pockets and should book ahead.

Hôtel Le Blason   Hotel €

(☑ 02 47 23 22 41; www.leblason.fr; 11 place Richelieu; s €53, d €53-66, q €88; ❄ @ ☎) Quirky, creaky budget hotel on a quiet square with 25 higgledy-piggledy rooms wedged around corridors: most are small, flowery and timber-beamed. Upstairs rooms under the eaves come with air-conditioning.

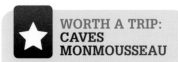

WORTH A TRIP:
CAVES MONMOUSSEAU

Sitting quietly under a dramatic 12th-century *donjon* (keep), Montrichard, 9km east of Chenonceau, offers a fizzy pit stop. Just outside town, the 15km-long Caves Monmousseau (🎫 02 54 71 66 64; www.monmousseau.com; 71 rte de Vierzon; ⏰ 10am-12.30pm & 1.30-6pm Apr–mid-Nov, 10am-noon & 2-5pm Mon-Fri mid-Nov–Mar) are carved into the tufa stone: a perfect 12°C environment for the local crémant (sparkling wine). A 45-minute tour (adult/child €3.50/free) explains winemaking methods and ends with a tasting.

Centre Charles
Péguy-Auberge de Jeunesse   Hostel €

(🎫 02 47 30 60 90; www.centrecharlespéguy.fr; Île d'Or; per person €19.50; @ 🛜) Efficient 72-bed, boarding-school-style hostel on Île d'Or, the peaceful river island opposite the château. Discounts for multi-night stays.

Camping Municipal
de l'Île d'Or   Campground €

(🎫 02 47 57 23 37; www.camping-amboise.com; Île d'Or; sites per adult/child/tent €3/2/3.80; ⏰ Apr-Sep; 🏊) Pleasant campground on Île d'Or. Facilities include pool, tennis courts, ping-pong and canoe hire.

⭐ Au Charme Rabelaisien   B&B €€

(🎫 02 47 57 53 84; www.au-charme-rabelaisien.com; 25 rue Rabelais; d incl breakfast €92-179; 🏊 🛜 🏊) At this calm haven in the centre, Sylvie offers the perfect small B&B experience. Mixing modern fixtures with antique charm, three comfy rooms share a flower-filled garden, pool and free enclosed parking. The spacious Chambre Nature is delightfully secluded and only a few steps from the pool. Breakfasts are fabs.

Le Vieux Manoir   B&B €€

(🎫 02 47 30 41 27; www.le-vieux-manoir.com; 13 rue Rabelais; r incl breakfast €160-200; 🏊 🛜) Set back in a lovely walled garden, this restored mansion is stuffed floor to ceiling with period charm. Rooms get lots of natural light, and owners Gloria and Bob (expat Americans

who had an award-winning Boston B&B) are generous with their knowledge of the area.

Le Clos d'Amboise   Historic Hotel €€€

(🎫 02 47 30 10 20; www.leclosamboise.com; 27 rue Rabelais; r €140-210, ste €210-295; 🏊 @ 🛜 🏊) Backed by a vast grassy lawn, complete with 200-year-old trees, a heated pool and parking, this posh pad offers a taste of country living in the heart of town. Stylish features abound, from luxurious fabrics to wood-panelling and antique beds. The best rooms have separate sitting areas, original fireplaces or garden-front windows.

Le Manoir Les Minimes   Design Hotel €€€

(🎫 02 47 30 40 40; www.manoirlesminimes.com; 34 quai Charles Guinot; r €139-225, ste €305-530; 🏊 @ 🛜) This pamper-palace would put most châteaux to shame. The best rooms in the main building have tall windows opening onto Loire or château views (corner suite No 10 has both!).

Château de Pray   Castle Hotel €€€

(🎫 02 47 57 23 67; www.chateaudepray.com; rue de Cedre; d €215-255, q €285) What better way to feel the Loire vibe, than to stay in a château? Rooms are sumptuous, bathrooms modern and grounds relaxing at this small château 3.5km northeast of Amboise. It also has a top restaurant (four-/five-course *menus* €57/70) open for lunch and dinner (closed December and January).

- - - - - - - - - - - - - - - - - -

🍴 Eating

⭐ Chez Bruno   Bistro €

(🎫 02 47 57 73 49; www.bistrotchezbruno.com; 38-40 place Michel Debré; mains €8-12; ⏰ lunch & dinner Tue-Sat) Uncork a host of local vintages in a lively contemporary setting just beneath the towering château. Tables of chatting visitors and locals alike dig into delicious, inexpensive regional cooking. If you're after Loire Valley wine tips, this is the place.

Bigot   Patisserie €

(🎫 02 47 57 04 46; www.bigot-amboise.com; place du Château; mains €6-11; ⏰ noon-7.30pm Mon, 9am-7.30pm Tue-Fri, 8.30am-7.30pm Sat & Sun) Since 1913 this award-winning *chocolaterie* and patisserie has been creating some of the Loire's creamiest cakes and gooiest treats: multicoloured macarons, handmade chocolates and petits fours, alongside savoury omelettes, salads and quiches.

La Fourchette   Traditional French €€

(☑ 06 11 78 16 98; 9 rue Malebranche; lunch/dinner menus €15/24; ☺ noon-1.30pm Tue-Sat, 7-9.30pm Fri & Sat) Tucked into a back alley behind the tourist office, this is Amboise's favourite address for straightforward home cooking. Chef Christine makes you feel like you've been invited to her house for lunch. It's small so reserve ahead.

Le Patio   Modern French €€

(☑ 02 47 79 00 00; www.facebook.com/lepatio amboise; 14 rue Nationale; menus from €29; ☺ noon-2pm & 7-9.30pm Thu-Mon) Pick a table either in the airy, modern interior or out in the bustling pedestrian rue Nationale, under the Tour de l'Horloge, and settle in with the locals for creative, beautifully presented French cuisine. Superb wine selection and friendly staff round it all out.

Self-Catering

Food Market   Food Market

(☺ 8am-1pm Fri & Sun) Fills the riverbank west of the tourist office.

- - - - - - - - - - - - - - - - - -

🍸 Drinking & Nightlife

Le Shaker   Bar

(3 quai François Tissard, Île d'Or; ☺ 6-11pm Tue, to 3am Wed-Sun) This low-key bar on the Île d'Or enjoys spectacular views of the château and the river from its Loire-side tables.

❶ Information

Tourist Office (☑ 02 47 57 09 28; www. amboise-valdeloire.com; quai du Général de Gaulle; ☺ 9.30am-6pm Mon-Sat, 10am-1pm & 2-5pm Sun, closed Sun Nov-Mar) Sells walking and cycling maps, plus discount ticket combinations for the château, Clos Lucé and the Pagode de Chanteloup, and offers walking tours. Amboise Tour is its free app. Located riverside.

Château de Villandry

Completed in 1756, one of the last major Renaissance châteaux to be built in the Loire Valley, the Château de Villandry (☑ 02 47 50 02 09; www.chateauvillandry.com; chateau & gardens adult/child €9.50/5.50, gardens only €6.50/4.50, audioguides €4; ☺ 9am-6pm Apr-Oct, earlier closing rest of year, closed mid-Nov–Dec) is deservedly famous for what lies outside the château, not what lies within. Encircled by tall walls, the château's glorious landscaped gardens (closing 30 minutes after the château) are some

of the finest in France, occupying over 6 hectares filled with painstakingly manicured lime trees, ornamental vines, cascading flowers, razor-sharp box hedges and tinkling fountains.

Try to visit when the gardens are blooming, between April and October; midsummer is most spectacular.

The original gardens and château were built by Jean le Breton, who served François I as finance minister and Italian ambassador (and supervised the construction of Chambord). During his time as ambassador, le Breton became enamoured with the art of Italian Renaissance gardening, and created his own ornamental masterpiece at his newly constructed château at Villandry.

Wandering the pebbled walkways you'll see formal water gardens, a maze, vineyards and the Jardin d'Ornement (Ornamental Garden), which depicts various aspects of love (fickle, passionate, tender and tragic) using geometrically pruned hedges and coloured flowerbeds. The Sun Garden is a looser array of gorgeous multicoloured and multiscented perennials. But the highlight is the 16th-century decorative potager (kitchen garden), where even the vegetables are laid out in regimental colour-coordinated fashion; plantings change in spring and autumn.

After the gardens, the château's interior is a bit of a let-down compared with others in the region. Nevertheless, highlights include an over-the-top oriental room, complete with a gilded ceiling plundered from a 15th-century Moorish palace in Toledo, and a gallery of Spanish and Flemish art. Best of all are the bird's-eye views across the gardens and the nearby Loire and Cher rivers from the top of the donjon (the only remnant from the original medieval château) and the belvédère (panoramic viewpoint).

Château de Langeais

Fantastically preserved inside and out, the Château de Langeais (☑ 02 47 96 72 60; www. chateau-de-langeais.com; adult/child €8.50/5; ☺ 9.30am-6.30pm Apr–mid-Nov, 10am-5pm mid-Nov–Mar) was constructed as a fortress in the 1460s to cut off the likely invasion route from Brittany. It remains every inch the medieval stronghold: crenellated ramparts and defensive towers jut out from the rooftops of the surrounding village. Original 15th-century furniture fills its flagstoned rooms.

Château d'Ussé

Among many fine Flemish and Aubusson tapestries, look out for one from 1530 depicting astrological signs; an intricate Les Mille Fleurs; and the famous Les Neuf Preux series portraying nine 'worthy' knights representing the epitome of medieval courtly honour.

In one room, an odd waxwork display illustrates the marriage of Charles VIII and Anne of Brittany, which was held here on 6 December 1491 and brought about the historic union of France and Brittany.

Up top, stroll the castle's ramparts for a soldier's-eye view of the town: gaps underfoot enabled boiling oil, rocks and ordure to be dumped on attackers. Across the château's courtyard, climb to the top of the ruined keep, constructed by the 10th-century warlord, Count Foulques Nerra. Built in 944, it's the oldest in France and fronts sprawling parks.

✕ Eating

Au Coin des Halles Bistro €€
(☑02 47 96 37 25; www.aucoindeshalles.com; 9 rue Gambetta; lunch/dinner menus from €16/26; ⏲12.15-2pm & 7.15-9pm Fri-Tue) The village of Langeais (population 4120), with its peaceful walking streets, is a fun pit stop in the midst of the mayhem of castle-hunting. The town's market bustles on Sunday mornings and you can dine at Au Coin des Halles, the village's elegant bistro.

🛈 Getting There & Away

Langeais is 14km west of Villandry and about 31km southwest of Tours. Its train station, 400m from the château, is on the line linking Tours (€5.60, 20 minutes, six to eight daily) and Saumur (€8.10, 25 minutes, six to 10 daily).

Château d'Azay-le-Rideau

Romantic, moat-ringed Château d'Azay-le-Rideau (☑02 47 45 42 04; www.azay-le-rideau.monuments-nationaux.fr/en; adult/child €8.50/free; ⏲9.30am-6pm Apr-Sep, to 7pm Jul & Aug, 10am-5.15pm Oct-Mar) is wonderfully adorned with slender turrets, geometric windows and decorative stonework, wrapped up within a shady landscaped park. Built in the 1500s on a natural island in the middle of the River Indre, the château is one of the Loire's loveliest: Honoré de Balzac called it a 'multi-faceted diamond set in the River Indre'.

Its most famous feature is its open loggia staircase, in the Italian style, overlooking the central courtyard and decorated with the salamanders and ermines of François I and Queen Claude. The interior is mostly 19th century, remodelled by the Marquis de Biencourt from the original 16th-century château built by Gilles Berthelot, chief treasurer for François I. In July and August, a son et lumière (sound-and-light show; adult/child €11/3), one of the Loire's oldest and best, is projected onto the castle walls nightly.

Audioguides (adult €4.50) are available in five languages, and 45-minute guided tours in French are free.

Château d'Ussé

The main claim to fame of elaborate Château d'Ussé (02 47 95 54 05; www.chateau dusse.fr; adult/child €14/4; 10am-6pm, to 7pm Apr-Aug, closed early Nov–mid-Feb) is as the inspiration for Charles Perrault's classic fairy tale *La Belle au Bois Dormant* (known to English-speakers as *Sleeping Beauty*).

Ussé's creamy white towers and slate roofs jut out from the edge of the forest of Chinon, offering sweeping views across the flat Loire countryside and the flood-prone River Indre. Its most notable features are the wonderful formal gardens designed by André Le Nôtre, lanscape architect of Versailles.

The castle mainly dates from the 15th and 16th centuries, built on top of a much earlier 11th-century fortress. You may be satisfied just looking at the château from outside, since refurbished rooms are starting to show their age. They include a series of dodgy wax models recounting the tale of Sleeping Beauty.

A popular local rumour claims Ussé was one of Walt Disney's inspirations when he dreamed up his magic kingdom (check out the Disney logo and you might agree).

Ussé is on the edge of the small riverside village of Rigny-Ussé, about 14km north of Chinon. There is no public transport.

Chinon

POP 8379

Peacefully placed along the northern bank of the Vienne and dominated by its expansive hillside château, Chinon is etched in France's collective memory as both the fortress of Henri II Plantagenet and the place where Joan of Arc first met Charles VII in 1429. Within the warren of the village's white tufa houses and black slate rooftops you'll discover an appealing medieval quarter.

Chinon is also renowned as one of the Loire's main wine-producing areas. Chinon AOC (www.chinon.com) cabernet franc vineyards stretch along both sides of the river.

You can park for free above town, access the fortress, and then take the free lift (7am-midnight Apr-Sep, to 11pm Oct-Mar) into the lower town (which has paid parking) to explore.

Sights

★ Forteresse Royale de Chinon
Fortress

(02 47 93 13 45; www.forteressechinon.fr; adult/child €8.50/6.50; 9.30am-7pm May-Aug, shorter hours rest of year) The hilltop site, with fabulous views across town and the river, is split into three sections separated by dry moats. The 12th-century Fort St-Georges (which houses the ticket booth and shop) and the Middle Castle with the Logis Royal (Royal Lodgings) remain from the time when the Plantagenet court of Henry II and Eleanor of Aquitaine was held here. Fort du Coudray sits on the tip of the promontory and has 13th-century Tour du Coudray, where Joan of Arc stayed in 1429, and which was used to imprison Knights Templar (find their graffiti inside).

When you initially enter the middle castle, you pass the 14th-century Tour de l'Horloge to reach the Logis Royal. Only the south wing remains of the Logis, and it is filled with interesting multimedia exhibits, a collection of Joan of Arc memorabilia, and area archaeological finds.

The castle has neat multimedia booklets that trigger film and audio in your native language throughout the site, as well as audioguides (€2.50).

★ Medieval Town
Historic Quarter

Author François Rabelais (c 1483–1553), whose works include the Gargantua and Pantagruel series, grew up in Chinon; you'll see Rabelais-related names dotted all around the old town, which offers a fine cross-section of medieval architecture, best seen along rue Haute St-Maurice and rue Voltaire. The tourist office has a free walking-tour leaflet and offers French-language guided tours (adult/child €4.70/2.50).

Look out for the remarkable Hôtel du Gouverneur (rue Haute St-Maurice), an impressive townhouse with a double-flighted staircase ensconced behind a carved gateway, and

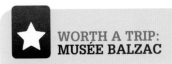

WORTH A TRIP:
MUSÉE BALZAC

Meander down the Indre Valley along the tiny D84, passing mansions, villages and troglodyte caves, and 7km east of Azay-le-Rideau you come to sweet Saché. Once home to American sculptor Alexander Calder (one of his mobiles sits in the town square), it still celebrates the life of long-time inhabitant Honoré de Balzac (1799–1850), author of *La Comédie Humaine*.

The lovely Musée Balzac (☑ 02 47 26 86 50; www.musee-balzac.fr; adult/child €5/4; ☺ 10am-6pm daily Apr-Sep, 10am-12.30pm & 2-5pm Wed-Mon Oct-Mar) inhabits the town's château where Balzac was a habitual guest of his parents' friend, Jean Margonne. On a quiet slope in the lush river valley, the castle features original furnishings, manuscripts, letters and first editions. Feeling the peace, you can easily imagine Balzac escaping his hectic Parisian life and reclining here in his cosy bed, a board on his knees, writing for 12 hours a day – as he did.
Nearby Auberge du XIIe Siecle (☑ 02 47 26 88 77; 1 rue du Château, menus €38-90; ☺ noon-1.30pm Wed-Mon, 7-9pm Mon-Sat) offers a gourmet country pit stop.

Touraine Fil Vert's bus I serves Saché.

the nearby Gothic Palais du Bailliage, the former residence of Chinon's bailiwick (now occupied by the Hostellerie Gargantua).

Caves Painctes de Chinon
Wine Cave

(☑ 02 47 93 30 44; www.chinon.com; impasse des Caves Painctes; adult/child €3/free; ☺ guided tours 11am, 3pm, 4.30pm & 6pm Tue-Sun Jul & Aug) Hidden at the end of a cobbled alleyway off rue Voltaire, these former quarries were converted into wine cellars during the 15th century, and written about by Rabelais. A brotherhood of local winegrowers, runs tours in summertime.

Chapelle Ste-Radegonde
Church

(☑ 02 47 93 17 85; rue du Coteau Ste-Radegonde; adult/child €3/free; ☺ 3-6pm Sat & Sun May, Jun & Sep, 3-6pm Wed-Mon Jul & Aug) Built into a cave above and 500m east of town, this atmospheric, half-ruined medieval chapel is noteworthy for its 12th-century Royal Hunt fresco and a staircase that descends to a subterranean spring associated with a pre-Christian cult.

Le Carroi Musée
Museum

(☑ 02 47 93 18 12; 44 rue Haute St-Maurice; adult/child €2/free; ☺ 2.30-6pm Fri-Mon mid-Feb–mid-Nov) Art and archaeology exhibits from prehistory to the 19th century relating to Chinon and its environs.

🛌 Sleeping

★ Hôtel Diderot
Historic Hotel €

(☑ 02 47 93 18 87; www.hoteldiderot.com; 4 rue de Buffon; d €70-100; ☎) This gorgeous shady townhouse is tucked amid luscious rose-filled gardens and crammed with polished antiques. The friendly owners impart the glowing charm you'd expect of a hotel twice the price. Rooms are all individually styled, from over-the-top Napoleonic to stripped-back art deco and have large flat-screen TVs. Breakfast (€9.40) includes a rainbow of homemade jams, plus locally produced apple juice, yoghurt and goat cheese. Parking is €8.

Hostellerie Gargantua
Historic Hotel €

(☑ 02 47 93 04 71; www.hotel-gargantua.com; 73 rue Voltaire; d €59-81; ☺ Apr-Sep; ☎) Harry Potter would feel right at home in this turret-topped medieval mansion. The simple, offbeat hotel has spiral staircases, pitch-dark wood and solid stone. Superior rooms are worth the cash, including Grangousier with its fireplace and four-poster, and Badebec with its oak beams and château views. Parking is €6.

Hôtel Le Plantagenêt
Hotel €

(☑ 02 47 93 36 92; www.hotel-plantagenet.com; 12 place Jeanne d'Arc; s €61-83, d €68-83, tr €94; ✳☎) A basic, dated but perfectly serviceable hotel halfway between the centre and the station, with rooms spread over three buildings. The original *maison bourgeoise* is more charming and less cramped than the motel-like annexe out back. Perks include guest laundry (€8), a pleasant patio and parking (€8).

🍴 Eating

Reserve ahead on weekends and during high season. Place du Général de Gaulle is loaded with sunny cafes.

★ Les Années 30
Traditional French €€

(📞 02 47 93 37 18; www.lesannees30.com; 78 rue Haute St-Maurice; lunch/dinner menus from €18/26; ⊘ 12.15-1.45pm & 7.30-9.30pm Thu-Mon) Expect the kind of meal you came to France to eat: exquisite attention to flavours and detail, served in relaxed intimacy. The interior dining room is golden-lit downstairs and cool blue upstairs; in summer dine under the streetside pergola, in the heart of the old quarter. The *menu* ranges from traditional duck *filet* to unusual choices such as crawfish tartare.

Restaurant au
Chapeau Rouge
Traditional French €€

(📞 02 47 98 08 08; www.restaurant-chapeau-rouge. fr; 49 place du Général de Gaulle; menus 3-course lunch €23, dinner €29-56; ⊘ noon-1pm Wed-Sun, 7.30-8.45pm Tue-Sat) There's an air of a Left Bank brasserie hanging around the 'Red Hat', sheltered behind red and gold awnings. Chatting families dig into hare fondant and other countrified dishes.

Self-Catering

Food Market
Market

(place Jeanne d'Arc; ⊘ morning Thu) There is a wide variety of produce available at the weekly market.

ℹ Information

Tourist Office (📞 02 47 93 17 85; www.chinon-valdeloire.com; 1 place Hofheïm; ⊘ 10am-1.30pm & 2-7pm May-Sep, 10am-12.30pm & 2-6pm Mon-Sat Oct-Apr) Free walking-tour brochure and details on kayaking, boat trips and hot-air balloons. Sells slightly reduced châteaux tickets. Occasional countryside bike tours. Free smartphone app. Its summer kiosk (⊘ 10am-1.30pm & 2.30-6pm Jun-Sep) is located up near the château.

ℹ Getting There & Away

Chinon is 47km southwest of Tours, 21km southwest of Azay-le-Rideau and 30km southeast of Saumur.

ANJOU

In Anjou, Renaissance châteaux give way to chalky white tufa cliffs concealing an astonishing underworld of wine cellars, mushroom farms and art sculptures. Above ground, black slate roofs pepper the vine-rich land from which some of the Loire's best wines are produced.

Angers, the historic capital of Anjou, is famous for its powerful dukes, their fortified hilltop château and the stunning medieval Apocalypse tapestry. Architectural gems in Anjou's crown include the Romanesque Abbaye de Fontevraud. Europe's highest concentration of troglodyte dwellings dot the banks of the Loire around cosmopolitan Saumur.

The area along the Rivers Loire, Authion and Vienne from Angers southeast to Azay-le-Rideau form the Parc Naturel Régional Loire-Anjou-Touraine.

Saumur
POP 28,558

There's an air of sparkly Parisian sophistication around Saumur, but also a sense of laid-back contentment. The food is good, the wine is good, the spot is good – and the Saumurites know it. The town is renowned for its École Nationale d'Équitation, a national cavalry school that's been home to the crack riders of the Cadre Noir since 1828. Soft white tufa cliffs stretch along the riverbanks east and west of town, pock-marked by the unusual artificial caves known as *habitations troglodytes*.

⊙ Sights

★ École Nationale
d'Équitation
Riding School

(National Equestrian School; 📞 02 41 53 50 60; www. cadrenoir.fr; rte de Marson, St-Hilaire-St-Florent; tours adult/child €8/6; ⊘ mornings Tue-Sat, afternoons Mon-Fri mid-Apr–mid-Oct, shorter hours rest of year) Anchored in France's academic-military riding tradition, Saumur has been an equine centre since 1593. Its École Nationale d'Équitation is one of France's foremost riding academies, responsible for training the country's Olympic teams and members of the elite Cadre Noir. Advance reservations are required for its one-hour guided visits (enquire about English-language tours), and the semi-monthly Cadre Noir presentations (adult/child €16/9) are not to be missed: they are like astonishing horse ballets. Check the website for dates and reservations.

You'll recognise members of the Cadre Noir by their special black jackets, caps, gold spurs and three golden wings on their whips. They train both the school's instructors and horses (which take around 5½ years to achieve display standard) and are famous for their astonishing discipline and acrobatic manoeuvres (like 'airs above ground'), which are all performed without stirrups.

Find the school 3km west of town, outside sleepy St-Hilaire-St-Florent. It's also the site of equestrian competitions.

Château de Saumur
Château

(☑ 02 41 40 24 40; www.chateau-saumur.com; adult/child €9/5; ☯ 10am-6.30pm mid-Jun–mid-Sep, 10am-1pm & 2-5.30pm Tue-Sun mid-Sep–mid-Jun) Soaring above the town's rooftops, Saumur's fairy-tale château was largely built during the 13th century by Louis XI, and has variously served as a dungeon, fortress and country residence. Its defensive heritage took a knock in 2001 when a chunk of the western ramparts collapsed without warning. After a decade-long restoration, the castle's porcelain collection reopened on the 1st floor. The 2nd floor is due to reopen soon; for now its impressive collection of vintage equestrian gear is housed in the adjacent abbey.

There's an **equestrian spectacle** (☑ 02 41 83 31 31; www.lesecuyersdutemps.fr; adult/child €19/15; ☯ Thu, Fri & Sat Jul & Aug) in summer which includes jousting, acrobatics and swordplay. Park in the lots up the hill from the château for free or walk up from town.

Musée des Blindés
Military Museum

(☑ 02 41 83 69 95; www.museedesblindes.fr; 1043 rte de Fontevraud; adult/child €8/5; ☯ 10am-6pm May-Sep, shorter hours Oct-Apr) Gearheads love this museum of over 200 tanks and military vehicles. Children can climb on some. Examples include many WWI tanks such as the Schneider and dozens of WWII models, such as the Hotchkiss H39, Panzers and an Issoise infantry tractor.

Musée de la Cavalerie
Museum

(☑ 02 41 83 69 23; http://museecavalerie.free.fr; place Charles de Foucauld; adult/child €5/3; ☯ 10am-noon & 2-6pm Tue-Fri, 2-6pm Sat-Mon) **FREE** Housed in the old military stables of the Cadre Noir, this museum traces the history of the French cavalry from 1445 in the time of Charles VII to modern tanks.

🏄 Activities

★ Maison des Vins
Wine Tasting

(☑ 02 41 38 45 83; www.vinsvaldeloire.fr; 7 quai Carnot; ☯ 9.30am-1pm & 2-7pm Mon-Sat, 10.30am-1pm Sun, closed Mon morning May-Sep, shorter hours

rest of year) For wine tasting and winery listings visit the Maison des Vins. Beautiful wine tasting drives include heading west along route D751 towards Gennes, or east on route D947 through Souzay-Champigny and Parnay. Or cut south of Angers over to Savennières.

Distillerie Combier
Distillery

(☑ 02 41 40 23 02; www.combier.fr; 48 rue Beaurepaire; tours €4; ☯ 10am-12.30pm & 2-7pm, closed Mon Oct-May, Sun Nov & Jan-Mar) In business since its invention of Triple Sec in 1834, this distillery has also resurrected authentic absinthe, the famous firewater. Taste these alongside other liqueurs including Royal Combier and Pastis d'Antan, and get a behind-the-scenes look at the production facility, with gleaming century-old copper stills, vintage Eiffel machinery and fragrant vats full of Haitian bitter oranges. There are three to five one-hour tours per day.

Langlois-Chateau
Wine School

(☑ 02 41 40 21 40; www.langlois-chateau.fr; 3 rue Léopold Palustre, St-Hilaire-St-Florent; tours adult/child €5/free, extended classes €225; ☯ tasting 10am-12.30pm & 2-6.30pm Apr–mid-Oct) Founded in 1912 and specialising in Crémant de Loire (sparkling wines), this domaine is open for reservation-only tours, tastings and a visit to the caves, and offers an introduction to winemaking.

👉 Tours

Croisières Saumur Loire
Boat Tour

(☑ 06 63 22 87 00; www.croisieressaumurloire.fr; adult/child €12/6; ☯ afternoons Jun-Sep, weekends May & Oct) Fifty-minute cruises from quai Lucien Gautier, across from Saumur's town hall.

Base de Loisirs Millocheau
Kayak Tour

(Pôle Nautique de Saumur; ☑ 02 41 51 17 65; www.polenautiquedesaumur.com; adult/child €28/22; ☯ office 9am-midday & 1-5pm Tue-Sat) Canoe and kayak tours on the Loire by reservation.

Carriage Rides
Carriage Ride

(www.attelages-cuzay.com; adult/child €8/5; ☯ 2-5pm Apr–mid-Oct) Tours depart from place de la République.

🛏 Sleeping

You'll need to reserve ahead for Saumur's high-calibre accommodation.

Hôtel de Londres
Hotel €

(☎02 41 51 23 98; www.lelondres.com; 48 rue d'Orléans; r €64-90, apt €95-130; ❄@🖥) Snag one of the refurbished rooms in jolly colours or one of the family-friendly apartments, all with big windows, gleaming bathrooms and thoughtful perks including afternoon tea (€3) and a well-stocked comic library. Parking is €5.

Camping l'Île d'Offard
Campground €

(☎02 41 40 30 00; www.saumur-camping.com; rue de Verden; sites for 2 people €15-25; ☺mid-Mar–mid-Nov; 🖥🏊) Well-equipped and very pretty campground on a natural river island opposite the château. Cyclists get discounts. Riverside and castle-view sites cost extra.

★Château Beaulieu
B&B €€

(☎02 41 50 83 52; www.chateaudebeaulieu.fr; 98 rte de Montsoreau; d incl breakfast €95-130, ste €140-200; 🖥🏊) Irish expats Mary and Conor welcome you to their sprawling home with a glass of bubbling crémant (sparkling wine), delicious homemade breakfasts and a wealth of friendly advice on surrounding attractions. Rooms are imaginatively and comfortably done up and the mood among gregarious clientele is one of extended family. Sun yourself by the pool or play billiards in the grand salon. Parking is free.

Hôtel Saint-Pierre
Historic Hotel €€

(☎02 41 50 33 00; www.saintpierresaumur.com; 8 rue Haute St-Pierre; r €95-200, ste €225-260; ❄🖥) Squeezed down a minuscule alleyway opposite the cathedral, this effortlessly smart hideaway mixes heritage architecture with modern-day comfort: pale stone, thick rugs and vintage lamps sit happily alongside minibars and satellite TV. Tiled mosaics line the bathrooms and black-and-white dressage photos enliven the lobby.

★Château de Verrières
Hotel €€€

(☎02 41 38 05 15; www.chateau-verrieres.com; 53 rue d'Alsace; r €170-260, ste €290-330; 🖥🏊) Each of the 10 rooms in this impeccably wonderful 1890 château, ensconced within the woods and ponds of a 1.6-hectare English park, is different. But the feel is universally kingly: antique writing desks, original artwork, wood panelling and fantastic bathrooms. Some, like the top-of-the-line Rising Sun suite (with a dash of modish Japanese minimalism), have views of the sun rising over the Saumur château.

✕ Eating

Saumur is one of the top culinary cities in the world; book ahead.

L'Alchimiste
Modern French €

(☎02 41 67 65 18; www.lalchimiste-saumur.fr; 6 rue Lorraine; menus €18; ☺noon-1.30pm & 7.30-9.30pm Tue-Sat) Clean flavours are the hallmark of this sleek family-run bistro. Seasonal ingredients sing out from a simple, constantly changing *menu*.

Bistrot des Jean
Bistro €

(☎02 41 52 44 07; www.bistrotdesjean.com; 19 rue de la Tonelle; menus lunch €12, 3-course dinner €20; ☺noon-2.30pm & 7-10pm Tue-Sat) Loaded with locals who appreciate the simple, traditional fare, this tiny bistro sits just off the waterfront on a small central walking street.

★Le Pot de Lapin
Modern French €€

(☎02 41 67 12 86; 35 rue Rabelais; tapas €5-7, mains €14-18; ☺noon-2pm & 7-9.45pm Tue-Sat) Jazzy music wafts from the cheery dining room through the wine bar and onto the streetside terrace as Chef Olivier works the tables, proposing perfect wine pairings and serving up tempting platefuls of ever-changing tapas and French classics. Somehow the vibe here is, simply put, happiness – happy staff, happy clients.

Start with a local bubbly then move on to perfectly seasoned shrimp *brochettes* (skewers), coulis-drizzled foie gras or pollock in parchment paper.

L'Escargot
Traditional French €€

(☎02 41 51 20 88; 30 rue du Maréchal Leclerc; lunch/dinner menus from €18/27; ☺noon-1.30pm Thu, Fri, Sun & Mon, 7.30-9.30pm Thu-Mon) A Saumur fixture for over half a century, this place is all about traditional recipes done really well, like escargots with garlic, parsley and 'three butters' (flavoured with herbs, walnuts and roquefort) or red mullet with fresh thyme, olive oil and vegetables.

L'Aromate
Modern French €€

(☎02 41 51 31 45; www.laromate-restaurant.com; 42 rue du Maréchal Leclerc; menus lunch €14, 3-course dinner €20-28; ☺noon-1.30pm & 7.30-9pm Tue-Sat) The newest entry on Saumur's hot culinary scene is buzzy and bright with changing *menus* that dare to mingle Asian and other influences with classic French cuisine.

★ LOCAL KNOWLEDGE: TOP LOIRE VALLEY WINES

Olivier Thibault merrily runs the excellent bistro Le Pot de Lapin (p81) in Saumur, dispensing delicious treats alongside a vast range of carefully curated wines. While he refuses to comment on who the top wine producers are in his nearby Saumur-Champigny area (too easy to make enemies!), he happily shares his favourites from elsewhere in the Loire. Look out for them on menus or in tasting rooms.

Domaine Philippe Gilbert (www.domainephilippegilbert.fr; Menetou-Salon) Excellent AOC (Appellation d'Origine Contrôlée) Menetou-Salon reds and whites from biodynamic *terroir* (land) north of Bourges.

Château Pierre-Bise (☑ 02 41 78 31 44; Beaulieu-sur-Layon) Claude Papin makes top Coteaux du Layon sweet whites, and Savenièrres and Anjou AOCs at his family's winery south of Angers.

Domaine de Bablut (www.vignobles-daviau.fr; Brissac-Quincé) Christophe Daviau produces superb organic reds under the Anjou Villages Brissac AOC.

Domaine Jaulin Plaisantin (www.jaulinplaisantin.com; Cravant-les-Côteaux) Top organic AOC Chinon by Yves Plaisantin and Sébastien Jaulin, 8km southeast of Chinon town.

Mikaël Bouges (☑ 02 54 32 79 25; michael.bouges@wanadoo.fr; Faverolles-sur-Cher) Organic Touraine AOC, from sparkling white and rosé to red, by a young vintner 3km south of Montrichard.

L'Amuse Bouche
Traditional French €€

(☑ 02 41 67 79 63; www.lamusebouche.fr; 512 rte Montsoreau, Dampierre-sur-Loire; menus lunch €17.50, dinner €29-37; ⊙ noon-1.30pm & 7.30-9.30pm Thu-Mon) Tuck into delicious, creative meals in a homey dining room or on the terrace in summer. Find it 5km southeast of Saumur on the D947.

★ Le Gambetta
Gastronomic €€€

(☑ 02 41 67 66 66; www.restaurantlegambetta.com; 12 rue Gambetta; menus lunch €25.50, dinner €32-99; ⊙ noon-1.30pm Tue & Thu-Sun, 7.15-9.45pm Tue & Thu-Sat) This is one to write home about: a fantastic regional restaurant combining refined elegance and knock-your-socks-off creative food. The parade of exquisitely presented dishes ranges from rosemary-and-thyme roasted pork with an asparagus-lemon-parmesan *maki* to surprisingly delicious wasabi crème brûlée. Some *menus* include wine pairings, and all are punctuated by surprise treats from the kitchen.

❶ Information

Tourist Office (☑ 02 41 40 20 60; www.saumur-tourisme.com; 8bis quai Carnot; ⊙ 9.15am-7pm Mon-Sat, 10.30am-5.30pm Sun mid-May–Sep, shorter hours rest of year; 🖥) Loads of info, transport schedules, slightly reduced châteaux tickets, smartphone app.

East of Saumur

Some of the region's most exquisite scenery stretches along the D947 east of Saumur, with sparkling riverside tufa bluffs and cave houses. Many of the renowned wine producers here offer free tastings from around 10am to 6pm from spring to autumn. Visit www.producteurs-de-saumur-champigny.fr for more information. The area is served by Agglobus line 1.

Turquant

Ten kilometres east of Saumur, the picturesque village of Turquant has one of the region's highest concentrations of troglodyte dwellings. Many have now been spiffed up and converted into shops, galleries or restaurants.

◉ Sights & Activities

La Grande Vignolle
Winery

(☑ 02 41 38 16 44; www.filliatreau.com; ⊙ 10am-6pm May-Sep) A domaine and tasting room in grand tufa caves.

Le Troglo des Pommes Tapées
Cave

(☑ 02 41 51 48 30; www.letroglodespommestapees. fr; 11 rue des Ducs d'Anjou; adult/child €6/3.50;

2-6.30pm Tue, 10am-12.30pm & 2-6.30pm Wed-Sun, closed mid-Nov–mid-Feb) One of the last places in France producing traditional dried apples known as *pommes tapées*. You can see displays on how it's done, sample the wares and buy some to take home.

🛏 Sleeping & Eating

Demeure de la Vignole Design Hotel €€

(☑02 41 53 67 00; www.demeure-vignole.com; 3 impasse Marguerite d'Anjou; d €130-155, ste €155-270; 🛜🏊) This upscale hotel has several richly decorated troglodyte rooms and suites, and a subterranean swimming pool.

L'Hélianthe Bistro €€

(☑02 41 51 22 28; www.restaurant-helianthe.fr; Ruelle Antoine Cristal; lunch/dinner mains €11/15; ⊙ noon-1.30pm & 7.30-9.30pm Thu-Tue Apr–mid-Nov, shorter hours rest of year) Tucked into a cliff behind the town hall, this bistro has a hearty menu revolving around countryfied flavours. Expect stews and 'ancient vegetables' (Jerusalem artichokes, beets, rutabagas etc).

Bistroglo Bistro €€

(☑02 41 40 22 36; www.bistroglo.com; Atelier 3, rue du Château Gaillard; mains €10-15; ⊙ noon-7pm Tue-Sat Mar-Oct; 🛜) Artisanal beers and local wines are the lead-in to fresh local food dished up with a cave-side smile.

Montsoreau

The Château de Montsoreau (☑02 41 67 12 60; www.chateau-montsoreau.com; adult/child €9/6; ⊙10am-7pm May-Sep, 2-6pm Apr, Oct–Nov, closed mid-Nov–Feb; 🅿) is beautifully situated on the edge of the Loire. It was built in 1455 by one of Charles VII's advisers, and later became famous thanks to an Alexandre Dumas novel, *La Dame de Monsoreau*. Exhibits explore the castle's history, the novel and the river trade that once sustained the Loire Valley. There are spectacular river views from the rooftop.

❶ Information

Parc Naturel Régional Loire-Anjou-Touraine Maison du Parc (☑02 41 38 38 88; www.parc-loire-anjou-touraine.fr; 15 av de la Loire; ⊙9.30am-7pm) The Maison du Parc provides maps and information on activities throughout the 2530-sq-km Parc Naturel Régional Loire-Anjou-Touraine, a regional park established to protect the landscape, extraordinary architectural patrimony and culture of this section of the Loire Valley.

Candes-St-Martin

Just east of Montsoreau, the village of Candes-St-Martin (population 229) occupies an idyllic spot at the confluence of the Vienne and Loire rivers. St Martin died here in 397, and thus picturesque Candes became a major pilgrimage point and bears his name.

For great views, climb the tiny streets above the church, past inhabited cave dwellings, for a higher-altitude perspective on the confluence, or head down to the benches and path along the waterfront.

◉ Sights & Activities

Collégiale St-Martin Church

This beautiful 12th- to 13th-century church venerates the spot where St Martin died and was buried in 397 (though his body was later removed to Tours).

CPIE Val de Loire Boat Tour

(☑02 47 95 93 15; www.bateaux-candes.org; Candes-St-Martin; adult €9-14, child €6.50-9; ⊙ Jul & Aug) Two traditional high-cabined vessels known as *toues* depart from Candes-St-Martin and cruise the convergence of the Loire and the Vienne rivers for one to 1.5 hours.

Fontevraud-l'Abbaye

◉ Sights

⭐ **Abbaye de Fontevraud** Historic Abbey

(☑02 41 51 73 52; www.abbayedefontevraud.com; adult/child €9.50/7, audioguide €4.50, smartphone app free; ⊙9.30am-6.30pm Apr–mid-Nov, 10am-5.30pm Tue-Sat mid-Nov–Mar, closed Jan) Until its closure in 1793 this huge 12th-century complex was one of the largest ecclesiastical centres in Europe. The extensive grounds include a chapter room with murals of the Passion of Christ by Thomas Pot. And keep a look out for the multi-chimneyed, rocket-shaped kitchen, built entirely from stone to make it fireproof.

But the highlight is undoubtedly the massive, movingly simple abbey church, notable for its soaring pillars, Romanesque domes and the polychrome tombs of four illustrious Plantagenets: Henry II, King of England (r 1154–89); his wife Eleanor of Aquitaine (who retired to Fontevraud following Henry's death); their son Richard the Lionheart; and his brother King John's wife, Isabelle of Angoulême.

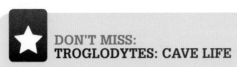

DON'T MISS:
TROGLODYTES: CAVE LIFE

For centuries the creamy white tufa cliffs around Saumur have provided shelter and storage for local inhabitants, leading to the development of a unique *culture troglodyte* (cave culture), as in the Vézère Valley in the Dordogne. The cool caves were developed into houses *(habitations troglodytes)* and even incorporated into castles, like Brézé. They are also perfect natural cellars for everyone from vintners to mushroom farmers. Many of the Loire's grandest châteaux were built from this dazzling stone.

Caves concentrate along the Loire east and west of Saumur, and around the village of Doué-la-Fontaine. Stop by the Saumur tourist office (p82) for a complete list. Bring something warm to wear as caves remain cool (13°C) year-round. The ones near Doué-la-Fontaine (a grim semi-industrial town) are best reached with your own wheels.

Rochemenier (☑ 02 41 59 18 15; www.troglodyte.fr; 14 rue du Musée, Louresse-Rochemenier; adult/child €5.70/3.30; ⊙ 9.30am-7pm Apr-Sep, 2-6pm Tue-Sun Oct-Nov & Feb-Mar) Inhabited until the 1930s, this abandoned village, 6km north of Doué-la-Fontaine, is one of the best examples of troglodytic culture. Explore the remains of two farmsteads, complete with houses, stables and an underground chapel.

Troglodytes et Sarcophages (☑ 06 77 77 06 94; www.troglo-sarcophages.fr; 1 rue de la Croix Mordret, Doué-la-Fontaine; adult/child €4.90/3.30; ⊙ 2.30-7pm daily Jun-Sep, Sat & Sun May) A Merovingian mine where sarcophagi were produced from the 6th to the 9th centuries and exported via the Loire as far as England and Belgium. Reserve ahead for a lantern-lit tour.

Les Perrières (☑ 02 41 59 71 29; www.les-perrieres.com; 545 rue des Perrières, Doué-la-Fontaine; adult/child €4.50/3; ⊙ 2-6.30pm Tue-Sun Apr-Oc) Former stone quarries sometimes called the 'cathedral caves' for their lofty sloping walls resembling Gothic arches.

Musée du Champignon (☑ 02 41 50 31 55; www.musee-du-champignon.com; rte de Gennes, St-Hilaire-St-Florent; adult/child €8/6; ⊙ 10am-6pm Feb, Mar, Oct & Nov, to 7pm Apr-Sep) Get acquainted with the fabulous fungus at the museum/producer tucked into a cave at the western edge of St-Hilaire-St-Florent.

Unusually, both nuns and monks at the abbey were governed by an abbess (generally a lady of noble birth retiring from public life). The abbey's **cloister** is surrounded by dormitories, workrooms and prayer halls, as well as a spooky underground sewer system and a wonderful barrel-vaulted **refectory**, where the monks and nuns would eat in silence while being read the scriptures.

After the Revolution, the buildings became a prison, in use until 1963. Author Jean Gênet was imprisoned here for stealing, and later wrote *Miracle de la Rose* (1946) based on his experiences.

Agglobus line 1 from Saumur comes to Fontevraud.

🛏 Sleeping & Eating

Fontevraud l'Hôtel Hotel €€

(☑ 02 46 46 10 10; www.hotel-fontevraud.com; d/q/ste €185/195/230; 🕿) Reopened in 2014 after a total renovation, plush rooms in muted siennas fill one of the abbey's priories. The gastronomic **restaurant** (⊙ noon-2pm Sun, 7.30-9.30pm nightly, closed Nov-Mar; menus €55-95) serves seriously haute cuisine, conceived by award-winning chef Thibaut Ruggeri.

Chez Teresa Tearoom €

(☑ 02 41 51 21 24; www.chezteresa.fr; 6 av Rochechouart; menus €12.50-17.50; ⊙ noon-7pm) Keeping up Fontevraud's English connections, this frilly little teashop and B&B is run by an expat English couple with a passion for traditional teatime fare: tea for two with sandwiches, scones and cakes costs €9.50. There are two upstairs rooms (double €60 to €65).

Château de Brézé

A unique Renaissance château, 12km south of Saumur, **Château de Brézé** (☑ 02 41 51 60 15; www.chateaudebreze.com; adult/child €11/6, tours free; ⊙ 10am-6.30pm Apr-Sep, to 7.30pm Jul & Aug, 10am-6pm Tue-Sun Oct-Mar, closed Jan) sits atop a network of subterranean rooms and passages dating from at least the 11th century that account for more square footage than the castle itself. Explore the original troglodyte dwelling directly under the château, then cross a deep moat to other caves adapted by the castle's owners for use as kitchens, wine cellars and defensive bastions. Finish your visit with a climb to the château's rooftop, followed by a tasting of wines from surrounding vineyards.

Agglobus line 2 connects Saumur and Brézé.

Angers

POP 151,161

This lively riverside city was the historical seat of the powerful dukes of Anjou and the Plantagenets and is now famous for its tapestries: the 14th-century *Tenture de l'Apocalypse* in the city's château and the 20th-century *Chant du Monde* at the Jean Lurçat museum. A bustling old town, with many pedestrianised streets and a thriving cafe culture, makes it an interesting western gateway to the Loire Valley.

◉ Sights & Activities

★ Château d'Angers   Château

(☎02 41 86 48 77; www.angers.monuments-nationaux.fr; 2 promenade du Bout-du-Monde; adult/child €8.50/free; ◷9.30am-6.30pm May-Aug, 10am-5.30pm Sep-Apr) This impressive black-stone château, formerly the seat of power for the counts and dukes of Anjou, looms above the river, ringed by battlements and 17 watchtowers. The star of the show is the stunning Tenture de l'Apocalypse (Apocalypse tapestry), a 104m-long series of tapestries commissioned by Louis I, Duke of Anjou, around 1375 to illustrate the Book of Revelation. It dramatically recounts the story of the Day of Judgment from start to finish, complete with the Four Horsemen of the Apocalypse, the Battle of Armageddon and the coming of the Beast.

Look out for graphic depictions of St Michael battling a seven-headed dragon and the fall of Babylon. The site has been inhabited since neolithic times and some ancient excavations remain.

Audioguides (€4.50) provide useful context, and guided tours are free. That black stone? It's actually called blue schist.

INFO: ANGERS CITY PASS

Swing by the tourist office to buy the Angers City Pass (24/48/72hr €14/22/29), good for entry to châteaux, museums, the Cointreau distillery, the tourist train and other sights, as well as for transport and parking discounts.

★ Musée Jean Lurçat et de la Tapisserie Contemporaine   Museum

(☎02 41 24 18 45; www.musees.angers.fr; 4 bd Arago; adult/child €4/free; ◷10am-6pm May-Sep, 10am-noon & 2-6pm Tue-Sun Oct-Apr) An excellent counterpoint to Angers' famous *Tenture de l'Apocalypse*, this museum collects fine 20th-century tapestries by Jean Lurçat, Thomas Gleb and others inside the Hôpital St-Jean, a 12th-century hospital founded by Henry Plantagenet, on the west bank of the river, north of the château. The centrepiece is the epic *Chant du Monde* (Song of the World), an amazing series depicting trials and triumphs of modern humanity, from nuclear holocaust and space exploration to the delights of drinking Champagne. Excellently curated rotating exhibitions.

★ Musée des Beaux-Arts   Art Museum

(☎02 41 05 38 00; www.musees.angers.fr; 14 rue du Musée; adult/child €4/free; ◷10am-6pm daily May-Sep, Tue-Sun Oct-Apr) The buildings of the sprawling, fantastic fine-arts museum mix plate glass with the fine lines of the typical Angevin aristocratic house. The museum has a section on the history of Angers and a superior 17th- to 20th-century collection: Monet, Ingres, Lorenzo Lippi and Flemish masters including Rogier van der Weyden.

★ Galerie David d'Angers   Museum

(☎02 41 05 38 90; www.musees.angers.fr; 33bis rue Toussaint; adult/child €4/free; ◷10am-6pm daily May-Sep, Tue-Sun Oct-Apr) Angers' most famous son is sculptor Pierre-Jean David (1788–1856), often just known as David d'Angers. Renowned for lifelike sculptures, his work adorns public monuments all over France, notably at the Panthéon, the Louvre and Père Lachaise cemetery. His work forms the cornerstone of this museum, housed in the converted 12th-century Toussaint Abbey.

Angers

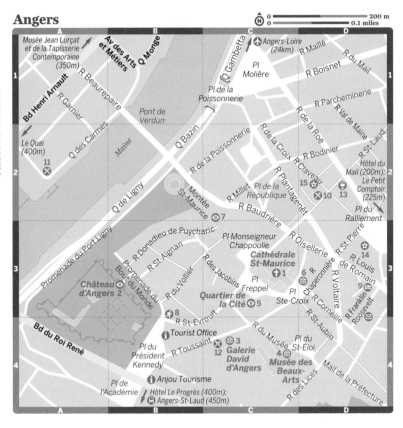

★ Quartier de la Cité

Historic Quarter

In the heart of the old city, **Cathédrale St-Maurice** (⊙ 8.30am-7.30pm) is one of the earliest examples of Plantagenet or Angevin architecture in France, distinguished by its rounded ribbed vaulting, 15th-century stained glass and a 12th-century portal depicting the Day of Judgment. Behind the cathedral on place Ste-Croix is the **Maison d'Adam**, one of the city's best-preserved medieval houses (c 1500), decorated with a riot of carved, bawdy figures. From the square in front of the cathedral, a monumental staircase, the **Montée St-Maurice**, leads down to the river.

Maison des Vins d'Angers

Wine Tasting

(⌨ 02 41 88 81 13; www.vinsvaldeloire.fr; 5bis place du Président Kennedy; ⊙ 2.30-7pm Mon, 10am-1pm & 2.30-7pm Tue-Sat) Head here for the lowdown on local Anjou and Loire vintages: tastings, sales, tours and tips.

🛏 Sleeping

Hôtel du Mail

Historic Hotel €

(⌨ 02 41 25 05 25; www.hoteldumail.fr; 8 rue des Ursules; d €71-91, tr/q €101/111; 🕿) Situated in a converted convent around a quiet courtyard, rooms have a light feel, even if they are a bit worn. The funky lobby, huge buffet breakfast (€10) and friendly staff make this a peaceful Angers base. No lift. Parking is €7. Find it on the eastern edge of the centre, near City Hall.

Hôtel Continental

Hotel €

(⌨ 02 41 86 94 94; www.hotellecontinental.com; 14 rue Louis de Romain; s €77-87, d €88-90; 🌢🕿) 🖉 Wedged into a triangular corner building in the city centre, this green-certified, metro-style hotel has 25 rooms decked out in cosy checks and sunny colours.

Angers

◎ Top Sights
1 Cathédrale St-Maurice C3
2 Château d'Angers B3
3 Galerie David d'Angers C4
4 Musée des Beaux-Arts C4
5 Quartier de la Cité C3

◎ Sights
6 Maison d'Adam D3
7 Montée St-Maurice C2

✚ Activities
8 Maison des Vins d'Angers B3

🛏 Sleeping
9 Hôtel Continental D3

✕ Eating
10 Chez Toi D2
11 Le Favre d'Anne A2
12 Villa Toussaint C4

◎ Drinking & Nightlife
13 Baroque D2

✪ Entertainment
14 Grand Théâtre d'Angers D3
15 Les Quatre-Cents Coups D2

Hôtel Le Progrès Hotel €

(☑ 02 41 88 10 14; www.hotelleprogres.com; 26 rue Denis Papin; s €52-60, d €69-90; 🛜) It's nothing fancy, but this reliable station hotel is solid, friendly and squeaky clean, and has a lift and free bike storage.

✕ Eating

Find student hangs and international restaurants radiating out from the rue St-Laud pedestrian area.

Chez Toi Bistro €

(☑ 02 41 87 85 58; 44 rue St-Laud; menus from €14; ⊙9am-12.30am Mon-Sat, 3pm-12.30am Sun; 🛜☑) Minimalist furniture and technicolour trappings meet in this zippy little lounge-bar, favoured by young Angevins. The front terrace along pedestrianised rue St-Laud is great for people-watching.

★ Le Petit Comptoir Bistro €€

(☑ 02 41 43 32 00; 40 rue David d'Angers; menus lunch €20, 3-course dinner €29; ⊙noon-1.30pm & 7.30-9.30pm Tue-Sat) Book ahead to ensure

a table at this ruby red, laid-back bistro dishing up delicious, beautifully presented French classics in a tiny dining room. Super wine list, too! Find it on the eastern edge of the centre, near City Hall.

Villa Toussaint French Fusion €€

(☑ 02 41 88 15 64; www.lavillatoussaint.fr; 43 rue Toussaint; mains €16-22; ⊙restaurant noon-2pm & 7.15-10.30pm Tue-Sat, bar noon-2am) With its chic dining room and tree-shaded deck, you know you're in for a treat at this buzzing bar and fusion restaurant, combining pan-Asian flavours with classic French ingredients. Reserve ahead.

Le Favre d'Anne Gastronomic €€€

(☑ 02 41 36 12 12; www.lefavredanne.fr; 18 quai des Carmes; menus lunch €25-35, dinner €45-95; ⊙noon-1.30pm & 7.30-9.30pm Tue-Sat) Muted tones, crystal, linen, and river and château views call for a romantic night out or a swanky lunch. Ingredients are always fresh (artichokes, asparagus, goat cheese, local fish) and the concoctions creative (a dash of cacao here and a splash of prune coulis there). No wonder it has a Michelin star.

Self-Catering

Food Market Market

(place Louis Imbach & place Leclerc; ⊙Sat morning) The weekly market spreads across two central squares: place Louis Imbach and place Leclerc.

🍸 Drinking & Entertainment

Cultural happenings appear in *Angers Poche,* a free weekly guide available at the tourist office. The best drinking street is rue St-Laud, which fills with folks of all ages.

Baroque Bar

(Barock Cafe; 35 rue St-Laud; ⊙3pm-2am) Streetside tables packed with students kick off the run of nightspots along the St-Laud pedestrian zone.

Grand Théâtre d'Angers Theatre

(☑ 02 41 24 16 40; www.angers-nantes-opera.com; place du Ralliement) Hosts theatre, dance and music.

Le Quai Performing Arts

(☑ 02 41 22 20 20; www.lequai-angers.eu; bd Henri Arnault; ⊙box office 1-7pm Tue-Fri, 3-6pm Sat) Angers' state-of-the-art performance and visual arts centre.

Château de Brissac
DEA/G. DAGLI ORTI/GETTY IMAGES ©

Les Quatre-Cents Coups   Cinema
(☑ 02 41 88 70 95; www.les400coups.org; 12 rue Claveau) Arts cinema showing non-dubbed films.

ℹ️ Information

Anjou Tourisme (☑ 02 41 23 51 51; www.anjou-tourisme.com; place du Président Kennedy; ⊙ 9.30am-12.30pm & 2-5.30pm Mon-Fri) Regional information.

Tourist Office (☑ 02 41 23 50 00; www.angers loiretourisme.com; 7 place du Président Kennedy; ⊙ 10am-6.30pm Mon, 9am-6.30pm Tue-Sat, 10am-6pm Sun, shorter hours Oct-Apr) Helpful, with lockers and loads of info on sights, activities and transport. Sells the Angers City Pass.

ℹ️ Getting There & Away

AIR

Angers-Loire Airport (ANE; ☑ 02 41 33 50 00; www.angersloireaeroport.fr) Seasonal flights to London and Nice. Located 24km northeast of Angers' centre.

Around Angers

South of Angers, the River Maine joins the Loire for the final leg of its journey to the Atlantic. The river banks immediately west of this confluence remain the source of some of the valley's most notable wines, including Savennières (near a pretty village of the same name) and Coteaux du Layon. The area due south of Angers, between Gennes, Brissac-Quincé and Savennières, makes for great, small-road exploration and rural driving.

Château de Brissac

The tallest castle in France, the Château de Brissac (☑ 02 41 91 22 21; www.chateau-brissac. fr; Brissac-Quincé; adult/child incl tour €10/4.50, gardens only €5/free; ⊙ 10am-12.15pm & 2-6pm Wed-Mon Apr-Oct, 10am-6pm daily Jul & Aug) comprises seven storeys and 204 rooms. Built by the Duke of Brissac in 1502, and still owned by the family, it is one of the most luxuriously outfitted castles in the Loire, with a riot of posh furniture, ornate tapestries, twinkling chandeliers and swank bedrooms – even a private theatre. Around the house, 8 sq km of serene grounds are filled with cedar trees, 19th-century stables and a vineyard, boasting three AOC vintages.

Four of the château's bedrooms are ridiculously extravagant *chambres d'hôte* (B&Bs; rooms €390).

Anjou Bus 5 (€1.80, 30 to 40 minutes, 11 daily Monday to Friday, five on Saturday) links Angers with Brissac-Quincé, 20km to the southeast.

Château de Serrant

Built from cream-and-fawn tufa and crowned by bell-shaped, slate-topped towers, the grand Château de Serrant (☑ 02 41 39 13 01; www.chateau-serrant.net; adult/child €10/6.50; ⊙ tours only 9.45am-5.15pm Jul & Aug, Wed-Sun & shorter hours rest of year) is a small slice of Renaissance style. Begun by aristocrat Charles de Brie in the 16th century, the château (seen only by guided tour) is notable for its 12,000-tome library, huge kitchens and an extravagant domed bedroom known as the Chambre Empire, designed to host Emperor Napoléon (who actually only hung around for about two hours).

The château is near St-Georges-sur-Loire, 15km southwest of Angers on the N23. Anjou Bus lines 22 and 24 serve Angers (€1.80, 30 to 40 minutes, two to four Monday to Saturday).

Burgundy

Two great French passions, wine and food, come together in Burgundy. And it's here, too, that you'll find some of France's most gorgeous countryside.

History

At its height during the 14th and 15th centuries, the duchy of Burgundy was one of the richest and most powerful states in Europe and encompassed a vast swath of territory stretching from modern-day Burgundy to Alsace and northwest to Lorraine, Luxembourg, Flanders and Holland. This was a time of bitter rivalry between Burgundy and France; indeed, it was the Burgundians who sold Jeanne d'Arc (Joan of Arc) to the English, and for a while it seemed quite possible that the kingdom of France would be taken over by Burgundy. In the end, though, it worked out the other way around, and in 1477 Burgundy became French. During the Middle Ages two Burgundy-based monastic orders exerted significant influence across much of Christendom. The ascetic Cistercians were headquartered at Cîteaux, while their bitter rivals, the powerful and worldly Benedictines, were based at Cluny.

ⓘ Getting There & Around

By car or rail (including the TGV Sud-Est), Burgundy makes an easy stopover on the way from the English Channel or Paris to the Alps or southern France.

From Dijon, autoroutes stretch northeast to Alsace (A36), north to Lorraine (A31), north and then west to Champagne (A31, A5 and A26) and south to Lyon and the Rhône Valley (A6).

Côte d'Or Vineyards

Burgundy's most renowned vintages come from the vine-covered Côte d'Or (literally Golden Hillside, but it is actually an abbreviation of Côte d'Orient or Eastern Hillside), the narrow, eastern slopes of a range of hills made of limestone, flint and clay that runs south from Dijon for about 60km. The exquisite terrain with its patchwork of immaculate hand-groomed vines is dotted with peaceful stone villages where every house seems to hold a vintner.

An oenophile's nirvana, the Côte d'Or vineyards are divided into two areas, Côte de Nuits to the north and Côte de Beaune to the south. The Côte de Nuits is noted for its powerful red wines, while the Côte de Beaune produces top-quality dry whites and delicate reds.

Côte de Nuits

The Côte de Nuits wine-growing area extends from Marsannay-la-Côte, just south of Dijon, to Corgoloin, a few kilometres north of Beaune. It includes the picturesque

FAST FACTS

» **Area** 31,582 sq km

» **Local industry** viticulture

» **Signature drink** white wine

villages of Fixin, Gevrey-Chambertin, Morey-St-Denis,Chambolle-Musigny, Vougeot, Vosne-Romanée and Nuits-St-Georges.

⊙ Sights

Château du Clos de Vougeot
Museum, Castle

(✐ 03 80 62 86 09; www.closdevougeot.fr; Vougeot; adult/child €7/2.50; ⊙ 9am-6.30pm Apr-Oct, 10am-5pm Nov-Mar, closes 5pm Sat year-round) A mandatory stop on your tour of Burgundy's vineyards, this magnificent wine-producing *château* (estate) provides a wonderful introduction to Burgundy's wine-making techniques. Originally the property of the Abbaye de Cîteaux, the 16th-century country castle served as a getaway for the abbots. Tours offer a chance to discover the workings of enormous ancient wine presses and casks.

Cassissium
Liqueur Factory

(✐ 03 80 62 49 70; www.cassissium.fr; 8 passage Montgolfier, Nuits-St-Georges; adult/child €8.50/6.50; ⊙ 10am-1pm & 2-7pm Apr–mid-Nov, reduced hours rest of year, last visits 1¾hr before closing) This museum and factory worships all things liqueur, with a particular focus on the blackcurrant, from which cassis is made. There's fun for the whole family: movies, displays, a 30-minute guided tour and a tasting with nonalcoholic fruit syrups for the kids. In the industrial area east of N74.

L'Imaginarium
Museum

(✐ 03 80 62 61 40; www.imaginarium-bourgogne. com; av du Jura, Nuits-St-Georges; adult incl basic/ grand cru tasting €8/15, child €5; ⊙ 2-7pm Mon, 10am-7pm Tue-Sun) An essential port of call on any wine-tasting itinerary, this gleaming modern museum is a great place to learn about Burgundy wines and winemaking techniques. It's fun and entertaining, with movies, exhibits and interactive displays, followed by tasting.

⚡ Activities

Wine Tasting
Wine Tasting

The villages of the Côte de Nuits offer innumerable places to sample and purchase world-class wines (especially reds) a short walk from where they were made. Wine can be bought direct from the winegrowers, many of whom offer tastings, allowing you to sample two or three vintages, but at many places, especially the better-known ones, you have to make advance reservations. Lists of estates and *caves* open to the public are available from local tourist offices.

You can also visit wine shops, including Le Caveau des Vignerons (✐ 03 80 51 86 79; place de l'Église, Morey-St-Denis; ⊙ 2-7pm Tue & Wed, 10am-1pm & 2-7pm Thu-Mon), which stocks most Côte de Nuits appellations and offers excellent advice, and Le Caveau des Musigny (✐ 03 80 62 84 01; 1 rue Traversière, Chambolle-Musigny; ⊙ 9am-6pm Wed-Sun), which represents more than 100 Côte de Nuits and Côte de Beaune winegrowers.

Walking
Walking

The GR7 and its variant, the GR76, run along the Côte d'Or from a bit west of Dijon to the hills west of Beaune, from where they continue southwards. The Beaune tourist office sells an excellent bilingual map, *Guide Rando Pédestre* (€3), which details 29 marked routes.

🛏 Sleeping

Maison des Abeilles
B&B €

(✐ 03 80 62 95 42; www.chambres-beaune.fr; 4 rue de Pernand, Magny-lès-Villers; incl breakfast d €68-75, q €125; 🖥🖳) New owner Céline maintains these five impeccably clean *chambres d'hôte* in Magny-lès-Villers, a small village off rte des Grands Crus, at the junction between Côte de Nuits, Haute-Côte de Nuits and Côte de Beaune. Rooms have colourful linen, and breakfasts are a feast of breads and homemade jams. The vast, flowery garden out back is another plus.

CLAUDE-OLIVIER MARTI/GETTY IMAGES ©

Château du Clos de Vougeot

Hôtel de Vougeot
Hotel €€

(☑ 03 80 62 01 15; www.hotel-vougeot.com; 18 rue du Vieux Château, Vougeot; d €82-123; 🖥) What's not to love in this gracious country manor? The 16 rooms are comfortable and impeccably maintained, many with rustically stylish features such as stone walls or exposed beams. Angle for one of the 10 rooms with a view of the Vougeot vineyards.

La Closerie de Gilly
B&B €€

(☑ 03 80 62 87 74; www.closerie-gilly.com; 16 av Bouchard, Gilly-lès-Cîteaux; incl breakfast d €85-90, tr €105, q €140; 🖥🖥🖥) Housed in a delightful 18th-century *maison bourgeoise* with a huge, flowery garden, this homey B&B has four spacious rooms, plus two apartments with kitchenette. English-speaking owner Sandrine offers wine tasting, wine classes and bicycles for rent. It's in Gilly-les-Cîteaux, just 1km east of Vougeot and only 15 minutes by train from Dijon or Beaune.

✕ Eating

Le Millésime
Modern Burgundian €€

(☑ 03 80 62 80 37; www.restaurant-le-millesime.com; 1 rue Traversière, Chambolle-Musigny; mains €19-28, lunch menu €19.50, dinner menus €29.50-49; ⏱noon-2pm & 7-9.30pm Tue-Sat) This renowned venture is located in an exquisitely renovated *maison de village*. The chef combines fresh local ingredients and exotic flavours in his excellent creations. Dark-wood floors, well-spaced tables and a warm welcome create an easy air.

Le Chambolle
Burgundian €€

(☑ 03 80 62 86 26; www.restaurant-lechambolle.com; 28 rue Caroline Aigle, Chambolle-Musigny; mains €14-17, menus €24-32; ⏱12.15-1.30pm & 7.15-8.30pm Fri-Tue) This unpretentious back-roads gem creates traditional Burgundian cuisine with the freshest ingredients. On the D122, a bit west of Vougeot in gorgeous Chambolle-Musigny.

Chez Guy and Family
Modern French €€

(☑ 03 80 58 51 51; www.chez-guy.fr; 3 place de la Mairie, Gevrey-Chambertin; menus lunch €24, dinner €28-45; ⏱noon-2pm & 7-9.30pm) Its dining room is large and light, and there's a tempting choice of dishes on its fixed-price *menus*. Along with tender duckling, signature seasonal specialities include rabbit leg and pollack. A long wine list backs up the food.

La Cabotte
Modern French €€€

(☑ 03 80 61 20 77; www.restaurantlacabotte.fr; 24 Grand Rue, Nuits-St-Georges; mains €15-21, menus €19.50-57; ⏱12.15-1.30pm & 7.15-9pm Tue-Sat) This intimate restaurant serves up refined, inventive versions of French dishes. No artifice or posing here, just excellent, if sometimes surprising, food.

ⓘ Getting There & Away

Transco (☑ 03 80 11 29 29; www.cotedor.fr) provides regular bus connections between Dijon and Beaune on its line 44, stopping in Nuits-St-Georges, Vougeot, Gevrey-Chambertin and other Côte de Nuits villages along the way.

Côte de Beaune

Welcome to one of the most prestigious wine-growing areas in the world. The Côte de Beaune area extends from Ladoix-Serrigny, just a few kilometres north of Beaune, to Santenay, about 18km south of Beaune. It includes the delightful villages of Pernand-Vergelesses, Aloxe-Corton, Savigny-lès-Beaune, Chorey-lès-Beaune, Pommard, Volnay, Meursault, Puligny-Montrachet and Chassagne-Montrachet, which boast Burgundy's most fabled vineyards. If you're looking for an upscale wine château experience, you've come to the right place.

⊙ Sights

★ Château de La Rochepot   Castle

(☑ 03 80 21 71 37; www.larochepot.com; La Rochepot; adult/child €4.50/2.50; ☉ 10am-noon & 2-5.30pm Wed-Sun) Conical towers and multicoloured tile roofs rise from thick woods above the ancient village of La Rochepot. This marvellous medieval fortress offers fab views of surrounding countryside and the interiors are a fascinating combination of the utilitarian (weapons) and the luxe (fine paintings).

Château de Meursault   Castle

(☑ 03 80 26 22 75; www.chateau-meursault.com; Meursault; admission incl tasting €18; ☉ 10am-noon & 2-6pm Mar, Apr, Oct & Nov, 10am-6.30pm May-Sep, 10am-noon & 2-6pm Sat, 10am-1pm Sun) One of the prettiest of the Côte de Beaune châteaux, Château de Meursault has beautiful grounds and produces some of the most prestigious white wines in the world. Particularly impressive are the 14th-century cellars.

Château de Pommard   Castle

(☑ 03 80 22 12 59; www.chateaudepommard.com; 15 rue Marey-Monge, Pommard; guided tour incl tasting adult/child €21/free; ☉ 9.30am-6.30pm) For many red-wine lovers, a visit to this superb château just 3km south of Beaune is the ultimate Burgundian pilgrimage. The impressive cellars contain many vintage bottles. If the tour has

whetted your appetite, you can sample Burgundian specialities at the on-site restaurant.

Château de Savigny   Museum, Castle

(☑ 03 80 21 55 03; www.chateau-savigny.com; Savigny-lès-Beaune; adult/child €10/5; ☉ 9am-6.30pm mid-Apr–mid-Oct, 9am-noon & 2-5.30pm rest of year) Drop in for wine tasting and stay to see the unexpected collection of race cars, motorcycles, aeroplanes and fire trucks. Last admission is 90 minutes before closing time.

⚘ Activities

Cycling   Cycling

The 20km **Voie des Vignes** (Vineyard Way), a bike route marked by rectangular green-on-white signs, goes from Beaune's Parc de la Bouzaize via Pommard, Volnay, Meursault, Puligny-Montrachet and Chassagne-Montrachet to Santenay, where you can pick up the **Voie Verte** (Green Way) to Cluny. Beaune's tourist office sells the detailed bilingual *Guide Rando Cyclo* map (€3).

Wine Tasting   Wine Tasting

You'll find plenty of wine-tasting opportunities in the wine-producing villages. You can stop at the famous wine châteaux or you may prefer to drop in at more laid-back wineries – look for signs.

⌸ Sleeping

★ Villa Louise Hôtel   Hotel €€

(☑ 03 80 26 46 70; www.hotel-villa-louise.fr; 9 rue Franche, Aloxe-Corton; d €98-195; @ 🖨 🖩) In the pretty village of Aloxe-Corton, this tranquil mansion houses elegant, modern rooms, each of them dreamily different. The expansive garden stretches straight to the edge of the vineyard and a separate gazebo shelters the sauna and pool. Genteel Louise Perrin presides, and has a private *cave,* perfect for wine tastings.

Domaine Corgette   B&B €€

(☑ 03 80 21 68 08; www.domainecorgette.com; 14 rue de la Perrière, St-Romain; incl breakfast d €90-110, tr/q €130/150; 🖨) The sun-drenched terrace at this renovated winery looks out on the dramatic cliffs. Tucked in the centre of the quiet village of St-Romain, its rooms are light and airy with crisp linen, and retain classic touches such as fireplaces and wood floors. Good English is spoken.

La Maison d'Olivier Leflaive
Boutique Hotel €€€

(☐ 03 80 21 37 65; www.olivier-leflaive.com; place du Monument, Puligny-Montrachet; d €170-200, ste €235; ⊘ closed Jan; ✳ @ 🛜) Occupying a tastefully renovated 17th-century village house in the heart of Puligny-Montrachet, this 13-room venture delivers top service and classy comfort. Best of all, it offers personalised wine tours and tastings.

🍴 Eating

Excellent restaurants are tucked away in the villages of the Côte de Beaune. Reserve ahead in high season.

Le Chevreuil – La Maison de la Mère Daugier
Modern Burgundian €€

(☐ 03 80 21 23 25; www.lechevreuil.fr; place de la République, Meursault; mains €23-36, lunch menu €21, dinner menus €24-59; ⊘ noon-1.30pm & 7.15-9pm Mon, Tue & Thu-Sat) Chef Tiago is known for his creative take on regional staples. The dining room's country-chic, with plenty of light, wood and stone for that down-home feel, and the menu takes the cream of traditional Burgundian and gives it a 21st-century spin. Try the *terrine chaude de la mère Daugier,* the house's signature offering, and you'll see what we mean.

La Table d'Olivier Leflaive
Bistro €€

(www.olivier-leflaive.com; place du Monument, Puligny-Montrachet; menus €25-30; ⊘ 12.30-2pm & 7.30-9pm Mon-Sat Feb-Dec) This is *the* address in Puligny-Montrachet. The trademark four-course 'Repas Dégustation' (tasting *menu*) combines seasonal French classics with global flavours. Add €25 and you'll sample a selection of five local wines chosen by the sommelier – a winning formula.

Le Cellier Volnaysien
Burgundian €€

(☐ 03 80 21 61 04; www.le-cellier-volnaysien.com; place de l'Église, Volnay; menus €18.50-29.50; ⊘ noon-1.30pm Thu-Mon, 7.30-9pm Sat) Solid Burgundian cooking in a cosy stone-walled, vaulted dining room in the heart of Volnay.

Le Charlemagne
Gastronomic Fusion €€€

(☐ 03 80 21 51 45; www.lecharlemagne.fr; Pernand-Vergelesses; lunch menus Mon, Thu & Fri €32-39, other menus €61-102; ⊘ noon-1.30pm Thu-Mon, 7-9.30pm Wed-Mon, closed dinner Wed Sep-May) Vineyard views are perhaps even more mind-blowing than the imaginatively pre-pared dishes melding French cuisine with techniques and ingredients from Japan. At the entrance of Pernand-Vergelesses.

Auprès du Clocher
Gastronomic €€€

(☐ 03 80 22 21 79; www.aupresduclocher.com; 1 rue Nackenheim, Pommard; mains €24-37, lunch menu €26, dinner menus €32-72; ⊘ noon-1.30pm & 7-9pm Thu-Mon) Celebrated chef Jean-Christophe Moutet rustles up gastronomic delights at Auprès du Clocher, in the heart of Pommard. The ingredients are Burgundian, but imagination renders them into something new and elegant. The wine list is superb.

Beaune

POP 22,620

Beaune (pronounced similarly to 'bone'), 44km south of Dijon, is the unofficial capital of the Côte d'Or. This thriving town's *raison d'être* and the source of its *joie de vivre* is wine: making it, tasting it, selling it, but most of all, drinking it. Consequently Beaune is one of the best places in all of France for wine tasting.

The jewel of Beaune's old city is the magnificent Hôtel-Dieu, France's most splendiferous medieval charity hospital.

☉ Sights

The amoeba-shaped old city is enclosed by thick stone ramparts and a stream which is in turn encircled by a one-way boulevard with seven names. The ramparts, which shelter wine cellars, are lined with overgrown gardens and ringed by a pathway that makes for a lovely stroll.

Hôtel-Dieu des Hospices de Beaune
Historic Building

(www.hospices-de-beaune.com; rue de l'Hôtel-Dieu; adult/child €7/3; ⊘ 9am-6.30pm) Built in 1443, this magnificent Gothic hospital (until 1971) is famously topped by stunning turrets and pitched rooftops covered in multicoloured tiles. Interior highlights include the barrel-vaulted Grande Salle (look for the dragons and peasant heads up on the roof beams); the mural-covered St-Hughes Room; an 18th-century pharmacy lined with flasks once filled with elixirs and powders; and the multipanelled masterpiece Polyptych of the Last Judgement by 15th-century Flemish painter Rogier van der Weyden, depicting Judgment Day in glorious technicolour.

Beaune

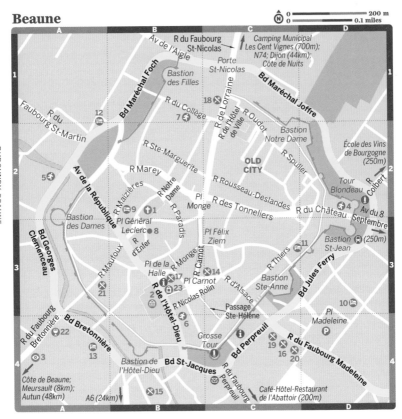

Beaune

◎ Sights
1 Basilique Collégiale Notre Dame	B2
2 Hôtel-Dieu des Hospices de Beaune	B3
3 Moutarderie Fallot	A4

◈ Activities, Courses & Tours
4 Bouchard Père & Fils	D2
5 Cellier de la Vieille Grange	A2
6 Marché aux Vins	B4
7 Patriarche Père et Fils	B1
8 Sensation Vin	B3

🛏 Sleeping
9 Abbaye de Maizières	B2
10 Chez Marie	D3
11 Hôtel des Remparts	C3
12 Hôtel le Foch	A1

13 Les Jardins de Loïs	A4

✖ Eating
14 Alain Hess Fromager	C3
15 Bissoh	B4
16 Caves Madeleine	C4
17 Food Market	B3
18 La Ciboulette	C1
19 Le Bacchus	C4
20 Le Comptoir des Tontons	C4
21 Loiseau des Vignes	A3

🍷 Drinking & Nightlife
22 La Dilettante	A4

🛍 Shopping
23 Athenaeum de la Vigne et du Vin	B3

Moutarderie Fallot   Mustard Factory

(Mustard Mill; ☏ 03 80 22 10 10; www.fallot.com; 31 rue du Faubourg Bretonnière; adult/child €10/8; ☻ tasting room 9.30am–6pm Mon-Sat, tours 10am & 11.30am Mon-Sat mid-Mar–mid-Nov, plus 3.30pm & 5pm Jun-Sep, by arrangement rest of year) Burgundy's last family-run stone-ground mustard company offers guided tours through its museum, focusing on mustard's history, folklore and traditional production techniques, with kid-friendly opportunities for hand-milling mustard seeds. An alternate tour focuses on Fallot's modern mustard production facility. Reserve tours ahead at Beaune's tourist office. Drop-ins can sample and purchase over a dozen varieties in the brand-new *dégustation* room.

Basilique Collégiale
Notre Dame   Church

(place Général Leclerc; ⊗ 9.30am-5.30pm) Built in Romanesque and Gothic styles from the 11th to 15th centuries, this church was once affiliated with the monastery of Cluny. It's notable for its extra-large porch and 15th-century tapestries. Tapestries are accessible by a €3 guided tour late April to mid-November only (schedules available at tourist office).

✈ Activities

Underneath Beaune's buildings, streets and ramparts, millions of dusty bottles of wine are being aged to perfection in cool, dark cellars. Wine-tasting options abound.

Marché aux Vins   Wine Tasting

(www.marcheauxvins.com; 2 rue Nicolas Rolin; ⊗ 10am-noon & 2-6.30pm, 10am-6.30pm Jul-Aug) Sample seven wines for €11, or 10 for €15, in the candle-lit former Église des Cordeliers and its cellars. Wandering among the vintages takes about an hour. The finest wines are at the end; look for the *premier cru* and the *grand cru* (wine of exceptional quality).

Bouchard Père & Fils   Wine Tasting

(www.bouchard-pereetfils.com; 15 rue du Château; tours €19; ⊗ 10am-12.30pm & 2.30-6.30pm Mon-Sat, 10am-12.30pm Sun) The atmospheric cellars are housed in a former medieval fortress and feature plenty of prestigious *grands crus* from Côte de Nuits and Côte de Beaune. Visitors taste three reds and three whites on the one-hour tour (offered in English at 4pm, in French at 3pm).

Cellier de la
Vieille Grange   Wine Tasting

(www.bourgogne-cellier.com; 27 bd Georges Clemenceau; ⊗ 9am-noon & 2-6.30pm Mon-Fri, 9am-noon & 3-6.30pm Sat, by appointment Sun) This is where locals come to buy Burgundy AOC wines for as little as €4.80 per litre. Tasting is free of charge.

Patriarche Père et Fils   Wine Tasting

(www.patriarche.com; 7 rue du Collège; audioguide tours €16; ⊗ 9.30-11.30am & 2-5.30pm) Spanning two hectares, Burgundy's largest cellars have 5km of corridors lined with about five million bottles of wine. (The oldest is a Beaune Villages AOC from 1904!) Visitors armed with multilingual audioguides can tour the premises in 60 to 90 minutes, tasting 13 wines along the way and taking the *tastevin* (tasting cup) home.

☞ Tours

The tourist office handles reservations for hot-air-balloon rides, and for vineyard tours (from €40) run by the following companies: **Chemins de Bourgogne** (☑ 06 60 43 68 86; www.chemins-de-bourgogne.com), **Safari Tours** (☑ 03 80 22 49 49, 03 80 24 79 12; www.burgundy-tourism-safaritours.com) and **Vinéatours** (☑ 06 73 38 37 19; www.burgundy-wine-tour.com).

Bourgogne Evasion   Walking, Cycling

(☑ 06 64 68 83 57; www.bourgogne-evasion.fr) Offers half-day, full-day and multiday cycling and walking tours through the vineyards.

Visiotrain   Tourist Train

(☑ 06 08 07 45 68; www.visiotrain2000.com; adult/child €7.50/4.50; ⊗ 11am-5.30pm, closed Wed & morning Sat) This small tourist train departs six times daily from rue de l'Hôtel-Dieu and tours the old town.

✵ Festivals & Events

Festival International
d'Opéra Baroque   Music Festival

(www.festivalbeaune.com) Held in July, this is one of the most prestigious baroque opera festivals in Europe. Performances are held at the Basilique Collégiale Notre Dame and the Hôtel-Dieu des Hospices de Beaune.

⊨ Sleeping

Camping Municipal
Les Cent Vignes   Campground €

(☑ 03 80 22 03 91; campinglescentvignes@mairie-beaune.fr; 10 rue Auge Dubois; sites per adult/tent €5.15/5.90; ⊗ mid-Mar–Oct; ☎) A flowery, well-equipped campground 700m north of the centre.

Café-Hôtel-Restaurant
de l'Abattoir
Hotel €

(☎ 03 80 22 21 46; 19 rue du Faubourg Perpreuil; r €29) If you don't need creature comforts and just want a central location at an unbeatable price, consider this unfussy hotel catering to local workers, with small, tidy rooms only a five-minute walk from the Hôtel-Dieu. Accommodation with half board (breakfast and dinner) is available (€39 per person). Note that reception is intermittently closed; call ahead.

Hôtel le Foch
Hotel €

(☎ 03 80 24 05 65; www.hotelbeaune-lefoch.fr; 24 bd Maréchal Foch; d €43-54, tr €66, q €82; 🖤) An acceptable plan B if others are full, this cheapie on Beaune's busy ring road has 10 basic but clean rooms. The cafe downstairs has plenty of local colour, though reception is often more gruff than welcoming, and wi-fi is undependable on the upper floors. There's free street parking out front.

★ Les Jardins de Loïs
B&B €€

(☎ 03 80 22 41 97; www.jardinsdelois.com; 8 bd Bretonnière; incl breakfast r €149, ste €180-190, apt €280-350; 🖤) An unexpected oasis in the middle of the city, this luxurious B&B encompasses several ample rooms, including two suites and a 135-sq-metre top-floor apartment with drop-dead gorgeous views of Beaune's rooftops. The vast garden, complete with rose bushes and fruit trees, makes a dreamy place to sit and enjoy wine grown on the hotel's private *domaine*. Free parking.

Chez Marie
B&B €€

(☎ 06 64 63 48 20; www.chezmarieabeaune.com; 14 rue Poissonnerie; incl breakfast d €85-115, tr/q €135/155; 🖤🚲) At this peaceful haven on a residential street only a five-minute stroll from central Beaune, Marie and Yves make visitors feel right at home, sharing conversation and travel-planning advice (especially for cyclists) over breakfast in the sweet central garden. The four rooms, including two family-friendly apartments with kitchenettes, are impeccably simple and airy. Bikes (regular and electric) are available for rent.

Hôtel des Remparts
Historic Hotel €€

(☎ 03 80 24 94 94; www.hotel-remparts-beaune. com; 48 rue Thiers; d €89-118, ste €135-159; ✳🖤) Set around two delightful courtyards, rooms in this 17th-century townhouse have redtiled or parquet floors and simple antique furniture. Some rooms come with exposed

beams and a fireplace while others have aircon. Most bathrooms have been renovated. Friendly staff can also hire out bikes. Parking is €10.

Abbaye de Maizières
Historic Hotel €€€

(☎ 03 80 24 74 64; www.hotelabbayedemaizieres. com; 19 rue Maizières; d €133-235, ste €280-370; ✳@🖤) Renovated in 2013, this characterladen four-star establishment inside a 12thcentury abbey oozes history, yet all 12 rooms have been luxuriously modernised. Some rooms boast Cistercian stained-glass windows and exposed beams; those on the top floor offer views over Beaune's famed multicoloured tile roofs. There's no lift, but the friendly staff will help haul your luggage upstairs.

✕ Eating & Drinking

Beaune harbours a host of excellent restaurants; you'll find many around place Carnot, place Félix Ziem and place Madeleine. Reserve ahead in high season.

Le Bacchus
Modern Burgundian €€

(☎ 03 80 24 07 78; 6 Faubourg Madeleine; menus lunch €14-16.50, dinner €26.50-33; ⊙ noon-1.30pm & 7-10pm) The welcome is warm and the food exceptional at this small restaurant just outside Beaune's centre. Multilingual co-owner Anna works the tables while her partner Olivier whips up market-fresh *menus* that blend classic flavours (steak with Fallot mustard) with tasty surprises (gazpacho with tomato-basil ice cream). Save room for splendid desserts such as Bourbon vanilla crème brûlée, flambéed at your table.

Le Comptoir
des Tontons
Regional Cuisine €€

(☎ 03 80 24 19 64; www.lecomptoirdestontons. com; 22 rue du Faubourg Madeleine; menus €29-42; ⊙ noon-1pm & 7.30-9pm Tue-Sat) Decorated in a hip bistro style, this local treasure entices with the passionate Burgundian cooking of chef Pepita. Most ingredients are organic and locally sourced. Does the beef with paprika taste better than the fat duck in aniseed sauce? You be the judge. Service is prompt and friendly.

Caves Madeleine
French €€

(☎ 03 80 22 93 30; 8 rue du Faubourg Madeleine; mains €14-24, lunch menu €23; ⊙ noon-1.30pm Mon, Tue, Thu & Fri, 7-9.30pm Mon-Fri) Focusing on fresh-from-the-farm meat and vegetables produced within a 100km radius of Beaune, this cosy little restaurant changes its menu daily. Reserve ahead for a private table, or enjoy a more convivial experience at the long shared table backed by wine racks.

La Ciboulette Burgundian €€

(☑ 03 80 24 70 72; 69 rue de Lorraine; menus €20-38; ☺ noon-1.30pm & 7.15-9.30pm Wed-Sun) Long popular with Beaune locals, but equally welcoming to tourists, this stone-walled, wood-beamed hideaway manages to feel both relaxed and refined, with smiling, efficient service and unpretentious but well-prepared dishes. Expect plenty of Burgundian classics, from pork cheeks in rich wine sauce to poached pears with cassis sorbet for dessert.

Bissoh Japanese €€€

(☑ 03 80 24 99 50; www.bissoh.com; 1a rue du Faubourg St-Jacques; menus lunch €13-23, dinner €37-78; ☺ noon-2pm & 7-10pm Wed-Sun) Take a break from Burgundy's high-calorie cuisine at this refreshingly simple, authentically Japanese eatery. The *menu* is anchored by classics (sushi, sashimi, grilled salmon, *tonkatsu,* imported sake) and bookended with fusion treats such as shrimp-studded *petit pois* soup or black sesame and green tea crème brûlée.

Loiseau des Vignes Gastronomic €€€

(☑ 03 80 24 12 06; www.bernard-loiseau.com; 31 rue Maufoux; menus lunch €20-28, dinner €59-95; ☺ noon-2pm & 7-10pm Tue-Sat) For that special meal with your significant other, this culinary shrine is the place to go. Expect stunning concoctions ranging from caramelised pigeon to *quenelles de sandre* (dumplings made from pike fish), all exquisitely presented. And even the most budget-conscious can indulge – lunch *menus* are a bargain. In summer, the verdant garden is a plus.

La Dilettante Wine Bar

(11 Faubourg Bretonnière; ☺ 11am-midnight Mon, Tue & Thu-Sat) This relaxed wine bar and gourmet grocery opened in 2013 and serves an excellent selection of wines along with soups, salads and Spanish-style *tapas* (small plates of cheese, Iberian ham and local charcuterie).

Self-Catering

Food Market Market

(Place de la Halle; ☺ 8am-12.30pm Sat) Elaborate weekly market. There's a much smaller *marché gourmand* (gourmet market) on Wednesday morning.

Wine tasting in Burgundy
OWEN FRANKEN/GETTY IMAGES ©

Alain Hess Fromager Cheese Shop

(www.fromageriehess.com; 7 place Carnot; ☺ 9am-12.15pm & 2.30-7.15pm Mon-Sat, plus 10am-1pm Sun Easter-Dec) This treasure trove of gourmet regional foodstuffs, including cheeses, mustards and wines, will tempt the devil in you. Don't miss the Délice de Pommard, the house's signature cheese. Also look for Burgundy's famous Appellation d'Origine Protégée (AOP) cheeses: strong, creamy, orange-skinned Époisses, invented by 16th-century Cistercian monks; and elegant little wheels of soft white Chaource.

🛍 Shopping

Athenaeum de la Vigne et du Vin Books

(☑ 03 80 25 08 30; www.athenaeum.fr; 5 rue de l'Hôtel-Dieu; ☺ 10am-7pm) Stocks thousands of titles on oenology (the art and science of winemaking), including many in English, as well as recipe books and wine-related gifts.

❶ Information

Tourist Office (☑ 03 80 26 21 30; www.beaune-tourisme.fr; 6 bd Perpreuil; ☺ 9am-6.30pm Mon-Sat, 9am-6pm Sun) Sells Pass Beaune and has lots of brochures about the town and nearby vineyards. An annexe (1 rue de l'Hôtel-Dieu; ☺ 10am-1pm & 2-6pm) opposite the Hôtel-Dieu keeps shorter hours.

ⓘ Getting There & Away

Near Beaune's train station, **ADA** (☎ 03 80 22 72 90; www.ada.fr/location-voiture-beaune.htm; 26 av du 8 Septembre) rents cars, scooters and bikes.

ⓘ Getting Around

Parking is free outside the town walls. There's a large, convenient free lot at place Madeleine, just east of the centre.

BICYCLE

Bourgogne Randonnées (☎ 03 80 22 06 03; www.bourgogne-randonnees.fr; 7 av du 8 Septembre; bikes per day/week €18/96; ☺ 9am-noon & 1.30-5.30pm Mon-Sat, 10am-noon & 2-5.30pm Sun Mar-Nov) Rents everything you need to explore the area by bike (bikes, helmets, panniers, baby seats, tandems) and offers excellent advice on local cycling itineraries.

Noyers-sur-Serein

POP 690

A must-see on any Burgundy itinerary, the absolutely picturesque medieval village of Noyers (pronounced 'nwa-yair'), 30km southeast of Auxerre, is surrounded by rolling pastureland, wooded hills and a sharp bend in the River Serein.

Stone ramparts and fortified battlements enclose much of the village and, between the two imposing stone gateways, cobbled streets lead past 15th- and 16th-century gabled houses, wood and stone archways and several art galleries.

Lines carved into the facade of the 18th-century mairie (town hall), next to the library, mark the levels of historic floods.

🕴 Activities

Noyers is a superb base for walking. Just outside the clock-topped southern gate, Chemin des Fossés leads northeast along the River Serein and the village's 13th-century fortifications, 19 of whose original 23 towers are extant. A few hundred metres beyond the last tower, climb the marked trail to Noyers' utterly ruined hilltop château, then follow signs to the Belvédère Sud for spectacular perspectives on the town and the valley below. There are also several longer hikes in the region; see the tourist office for details.

✵ Festivals & Events

For two weeks in July, various venues host classical concerts and jazz sessions during the Rencontres Musicales de Noyers (www.musicalesdenoyers.com).

🛏 Sleeping & Eating

Moulin de la Roche   B&B €

(☎ 03 86 82 68 13; facqarch@wanadoo.fr; rte d'Auxerre; s/d/tr/q incl breakfast €65/90/110/140; ☎ 🖶) Northwest of town, this renovated mill on three gorgeous hectares beside the River Serein has two beautiful guest rooms and a millwheel in the living room.

La Vieille Tour   B&B €

(☎ 03 86 82 87 69; place du Grenier à Sel; incl breakfast s €50, d €60-80; ☺ Apr-Sep; ☎ 🖶) In a rambling 17th-century house, this Dutch-run venture has several simply furnished *chambres d'hôte* of varying size, loads of local colour and a cheerful garden. The best rooms, in a round medieval stone tower, have dreamy river views.

★ Le Tabellion   B&B €€

(☎ 03 86 82 62 26, 06 86 08 39 92; www.noyers-tabellion.fr; 5 rue du Jeu de Paume; d €90-92; ☎) Friendly, knowledgable and multilingual owner Rita Florin runs this attractive B&B in a former notary's office right next to the church. The three tastefully furnished and charmingly rustic rooms are rife with personality, and there's a delightful garden at the back.

Restaurant La Vieille Tour   Modern Burgundian €€

(☎ 03 86 82 87 36; rue Porte Peinte; menus €17-25; ☺ noon-2pm Sat-Wed, 7-9pm Fri-Wed Apr-Sep; 🍴) Just beyond the clock tower at the town entrance, creative young chefs Laurens and Hélène serve a delicious, unpretentious and ever-changing *menu* of Burgundian staples and exotic interpretations. Vegetarian options are also available.

Les Millésimes   Burgundian €€

(☎ 03 86 82 82 16; www.maison-paillot.com; 14 place de l'Hôtel de Ville; menu €27; ☺ noon-3pm Tue-Sun, 7-9pm Tue-Sat) This culinary haven in a meticulously restored medieval house complete with a large fireplace and sturdy wooden tables specialises in *terroir* creations ranging from *jambon au chablis* (ham flavoured with Chablis wine) to *tourte à l'Époisses* (pie with Époisses cheese). It's also renowned for its respectable wine list.

🛍 Shopping

Noyers has a sizeable population of local and expatriate artists.

Création Maroquinerie
Leather

(📞 03 86 75 94 60; 24 place de l'Hôtel de Ville; ⊙10am-12.30pm & 2.30-6pm Wed-Sun) Among the town's quirky galleries is Création Maroquinerie, a fantastic leather shop full of chic belts and supple handbags. The proprietors, Yazmhil and Brice, do custom work and make everything on-site.

Illuminated Painting Studio
Illuminations

(📞 06 47 99 26 44; www.diane-calvert.com; 47 rue de la Petite Étape aux Vins; ⊙by appointment May-Sep) An interesting spot is Diane Calvert's illuminated painting studio where she grinds her own pigments from semi-precious stones and uses parchment and quill pens.

Maison Paillot
Food, Wine

(📞 03 86 82 82 16; www.maison-paillot.com; 14 place de l'Hôtel de Ville; ⊙9am-12.30pm & 3-7pm) Food and wine lovers should head for Maison Paillot, which combines a charcuterie/deli with a well-stocked wine cellar.

❶ Information

Tourist Office (📞 03 86 82 66 06; www.noyers-et-tourisme.com; 22 place de l'Hôtel de Ville; ⊙10am-1pm & 2-6pm, closed Sun Oct-May)

Vézelay

POP 440

The tiny hilltop village of Vézelay, a Unesco World Heritage Site, is one of France's architectural gems. Perched on a rocky spur crowned by a medieval basilica and surrounded by a sublime patchwork of vineyards, sunflower fields and cows, Vézelay seems to have been lifted from another age.

One of the main pilgrimage routes to Santiago de Compostela in Spain starts here (see www.compostelle.asso.fr).

History

Thanks to the relics of St Mary Magdalene, Vézelay's Benedictine monastery became an important pilgrimage site in the 11th and 12th centuries. St Bernard, leader of the Cistercian order, preached the Second Crusade here in 1146. King Philip Augustus of France and King Richard the Lionheart of England met up here in 1190 before setting out on the Third Crusade.

Vézelay's vineyards, founded in Gallo-Roman times, were wiped out in the late 1800s by phylloxera and were only re-established in 1973.

👁 Sights

⭐ Basilique Ste-Madeleine
Landmark, Church

(www.basiliquedevezelay.org) Founded in the 880s on a former Roman and Carolingian site, Vézelay's stunning hilltop basilica was rebuilt between the 11th and 13th centuries. On the famous 12th-century tympanum, visible from the narthex (enclosed porch), Romanesque carvings show an enthroned Jesus radiating his holy spirit to the apostles. The nave has typically Romanesque round arches and detailed capitals, while the transept and choir (1185) have Gothic ogival arches. The mid-12th-century crypt houses a reliquary reputedly containing one of Mary Magdalene's bones.

The church has had a turbulent history. Damaged by the great fire of 1120, trashed by the Huguenots in 1569, desecrated during the Revolution and repeatedly struck by lightning, by the mid-1800s it was on the point of collapse. In 1840 the architect Viollet-le-Duc undertook the daunting task of rescuing the structure. His work helped Vézelay, previously a ghost town, spring back to life.

Visitors are welcome to observe prayers or Mass. Concerts of sacred music are held in the nave from June to September; the tourist office and its website have details.

⭐ Musée Zervos
Art Museum

(📞 03 86 32 39 26; www.musee-zervos.fr; rue St-Étienne; adult/child €3/free; ⊙10am-6pm Wed-Mon mid-Mar–mid-Nov, daily Jul & Aug) This fantastic museum in the exquisite townhouse of Nobel Prize–winning pacifist writer Romain Rolland (1866–1944) holds the collection of Christian Zervos (1889–1970), an art critic, gallerist and friend of many modern art luminaries. He and his wife, Yvonne, collected paintings, sculptures and mobiles by Calder, Giacometti, Kandinsky, Léger, Mirò and Picasso (for whom he created a pivotal 22-volume catalogue).

Vineyards around Vézelay

Maison Jules Roy — Historic Building

(☑ 03 86 33 35 01; rue des Écoles; ☺ 2-6pm Wed-Sun, 2-5pm Mon, closed mid-Nov–mid-Mar) **FREE** Up near the top of town, the house of Jules Roy (1907–2000) sits in the shadow of the basilica. Walk around his beautiful gardens and see the Algerian-born writer's study.

🏃 Activities

Walking Trails — Walking

The park behind the Basilique Ste-Madeleine affords wonderful views of the Vallée de Cure and nearby villages. A dirt road leads north to the old and new cemeteries. Promenade des Fossés circumnavigates Vézelay's medieval ramparts. A footpath with fine views of the basilica links Porte Neuve, on the northern side of the ramparts, with the village of Asquins (pronounced 'ah-kah') and the River Cure. The GR13 trail passes by Vézelay.

AB Loisirs — Outdoor Activities

(☑ 03 86 33 38 38; www.abloisirs.com; rue Gravier, St-Père; ☺ 9.30am-6pm Jul & Aug, phone ahead rest of year) A few kilometres southeast of Vézelay in St-Père, this well-established outfit rents bikes (€25 per day) and leads outdoor activities such as kayak trips (8/18km from €23/38), rafting (€49), cave exploration (half day €39), rock-climbing (half day €37) and horse riding (per hour €18). Bikes can be brought to your hotel. It's best to phone ahead.

🎊 Festivals & Events

Rencontres Musicales de Vézelay — Music Festival

(www.rencontresmusicalesdevezelay.com) This not-to-be-missed festival of classical music is held at various venues in late August.

Cité de la Voix Summer Concert Series — Performing Arts

(www.region-bourgogne.fr/cite-de-la-voix) Vézelay's academy of vocal music stages free concerts in the basilica and elsewhere around town from late June through September.

🛏 Sleeping

★ Centre Ste-Madeleine — Hostel €

(☑ 03 86 33 22 14; centre.saintemadeleine@orange.fr; 26 rue St-Pierre; dm/s/d €16/23/40) First and foremost a pilgrims' hostel, this welcoming, well-run place reopened in 2013 after a major renovation. There are two large shared dorms, plus private rooms ranging from a four-bed family room to a cosy single-bed eyrie tucked under the eaves. The location directly across from the basilica is unbeatable, and guests have access to a well-equipped shared kitchen.

Cabalus — Historic Hotel €

(☑ 03 86 33 20 66; www.cabalus.com; rue St-Pierre; d €38-58) An incredibly atmospheric place to stay, Cabalus has four spacious rooms in a 12th-century building right next to the cathedral. They're sparsely decorated but come with sturdy beams, ancient tiles and stone walls. Note that the cheaper rooms have shared toilets. Organic breakfasts (€9) are served at the cafe downstairs.

Auberge de Jeunesse et
Camping de l'Ermitage
Campground, Hostel €

(☑ 03 86 33 24 18; www.camping-auberge-vezelay.com; rue de l'Étang; dm €16, sites per adult/child/car €3/1.50/1; ☺ camping Apr-Oct, hostel year-round) If being right in town isn't a must, this well-maintained venture 1km south of Vézelay is manna from heaven for thrifty visitors. After an extensive renovation in 2012, it now shelters well-equipped four- to 10-bed dorms with individual kitchenettes and gleaming en-suite bathrooms, flanked by a spacious, grassy camping area.

La Terrasse
Hotel €€

(☑ 03 86 33 25 50; www.laterrasse-vezelay.com; 2 place de la Basilique; r €100-150; ☎) Completely renovated in 2014, this six-room hotel enjoys a plum position opposite the basilica, complemented by numerous modern amenities – top-quality bedding, sparkling new bathroom fixtures and large flat-screen TVs. Unique touches include the direct basilica views from the bathtub in room 2 and the 12th-century stone window frame above the bed in room 4. Downstairs there's a terrace restaurant.

✕ Eating

À la Fortune du Pot
Burgundian €

(☑ 03 86 33 32 56; www.fortunedupot.com; 6 place du Champ du Foire; menus €16-24; ☺ noon-2pm & 7-9pm) Well-placed in the square at the foot of Vézelay's main street, this French-Colombian-run restaurant with English iPad menus is at its best in sunny weather, when tables spill out onto the terrace. A €16 three-course *menu* featuring Burgundian classics such as escargots, *tarte à l'Époisses* (Époisses cheese tart) and bœuf bourguignon is available for dinner as well as lunch.

Le Bougainville
Traditional French €€

(☑ 03 86 33 27 57; 26 rue St-Etienne; menus €27-32.50; ☺ noon-2pm & 7-9pm Thu-Mon; ☑) The smiling owner serves rich French and Burgundian specialities such as Charolais beef and tripe sausages. If you're growing weary of heavy regional dishes, fear not – Le Bougainville is also noted for its *Menu du Jardinier* (€27), which features vegetarian options – a rarity in Burgundy!

🛍 Shopping

Vézelay has long attracted artists and writers. About half a dozen art galleries and several wine and crafts shops line rue St-Pierre and rue St-Étienne.

Domaine Maria Cuny
Wine

(☑ 03 86 32 38 50; www.viti-culture.com; 34 rue St-Étienne; ☺ by appointment) At their store on Vézelay's main street, this family-run winery sells organic white wines from the tiny Bourgogne-Vézelay appellation. Owner Maria and her friendly daughter Julie can also organise vineyard tours in the region.

ℹ Information

Tourist Office (☑ 03 86 33 23 69; www.vezelaytourisme.com; 12 rue St-Étienne; ☺ 10am-1pm & 2-6pm, closed Thu Oct-May & Sun Nov-Easter; ☎) Sells hiking maps. Offers internet access (€2 per 10 minutes) and free wi-fi.

ℹ Getting There & Away

Vézelay is 15km from Avallon (19km if you take the gorgeous D427 via Pontaubert). The Clos car park 250m east of place du Champ-de-Foire (towards Avallon) is free; others at the base of town, behind the basilica and west towards Clamecy cost €3 to €4 per day.

Autun

POP 15,760

Autun is a low-key town, but almost two millennia ago (when it was known as Augustodunum) it was one of the most important cities in Roman Gaul, boasting 6km of ramparts, four monumental gates, two theatres, an amphitheatre and a system of aqueducts. Beginning in AD 269, the city was repeatedly sacked by barbarian tribes and its fortunes declined, but things improved considerably in the Middle Ages, making it possible to construct an impressive cathedral. The hilly area around Cathédrale St-Lazare, reached via narrow cobblestone streets, is known as the old city. If you have a car, Autun is an excellent base for exploring the southern parts of the Parc Naturel Régional du Morvan.

⊙ Sights

Napoléon Bonaparte and his brothers Joseph and Lucien studied in Autun as teenagers. Their old Jesuit college is now a high school called Lycée Joseph Bonaparte, on the west side of Champ de Mars. A small train (adult/child €7/3.50) offers guided town tours in July and August; contact the tourist office.

★ Cathédrale St-Lazare   Cathedral

(place du Terreau; ⊘ cathedral 8am-7pm Sep-Jun, plus 9-11pm Jul & Aug, chapter room summer months only) Originally Romanesque, this cathedral was built in the 12th century to house the sacred relics of St Lazarus. Over the main doorway, the famous Romanesque tympanum shows the Last Judgment surrounded by zodiac signs, carved in the 1130s by Gislebertus, whose name is inscribed below Jesus' right foot. Ornamental capitals by Gislebertus and his school, described in a multilingual handout, adorn the columns of the nave; several especially exquisite capitals are displayed at eye level upstairs in the Chapter Room.

Later additions include the 15th- to 16th-century bell tower over the transept and the 19th-century towers over the entrance.

Musée Rolin   Museum

(☑ 03 85 52 09 76; 3 rue des Bancs; adult/child €5.20/free; ⊘ 9.30am-noon & 1.30-6pm Wed-Mon) Don't miss this superb collection of Gallo-Roman artefacts; 12th-century Romanesque art, including the *Temptation of Eve* by Gislebertus; and 15th-century paintings such as the *Autun Virgin* by the Maître de Moulins. Modern art includes work by Maurice Denis, Jean Dubuffet and Joan Miró.

Roman Gates   Ruin

At the edge of town you'll find the impressive remains of two of Augustodunum's four Roman gates. The northern Porte d'Arroux was constructed during Constantine's reign, wholly without mortar. It supports four semicircular arches of the sort that put the 'Roman' in Romanesque: two for vehicles and two for pedestrians. East of town, Porte St-André is similar in general design.

Temple de Janus   Archaeological Site

(www.temple-de-janus.net) Long associated (wrongly) with the Roman God Janus, this 24m-high temple in the middle of farmland 800m north of the train station is thought to have been a site for Celtic worship. Only two of its massive walls still stand.

Théâtre Romain   Archaeological Site

(Roman Theatre; ⊘ 24hr) Let your imagination run wild at this ancient theatre designed to hold 16,000 people; try picturing the place filled with cheering (or jeering), toga-clad spectators. From the top look southwest to see the Pierre de Couhard (Rock of Couhard), the 27m-high remains of a Gallo-Roman pyramid that was probably a tomb.

☆ Activities

For a stroll along the city walls (part-Roman but mostly medieval), walk from av du Morvan south to the 12th-century Tour des Ursulines and follow the walls to the northeast. The Chemin des Manies leads out to the Pierre de Couhard, where you can pick up the Circuit des Gorges, three marked forest trails ranging from 4.7km to 11.5km (IGN map 2925 O).

The water-sports centre based at Plan d'Eau du Vallon (an artificial lake east of the centre) rents kayaks, paddle boats and bikes.

⨭ Sleeping

★ Maison Sainte-Barbe   B&B €

(☑ 03 85 86 24 77; www.maisonsaintebarbe.com; 7 place Sainte-Barbe; s/d €75/80, ste €120-140; ☎) Smack in the old city in a 15th-century townhouse, this colourful, spotless B&B has five spacious, light-filled rooms, including one with fine views of the cathedral and a two-bedroom suite that's perfect for families. The icing on the cake? The friendly, knowledgable owners prepare delicious breakfasts, and there's a verdant courtyard out back.

Les Arcades   Hotel €

(☑ 03 85 52 30 03; www.hotel-arcades-autun.com; 22 av de la République; s €40-43, d €50-53; ☎) Opposite the railway station, Les Arcades is a passable plan B if others are full, but don't expect the Ritz – rooms are unmemorable and service is lackadaisical. Parking costs €5.

★ Moulin Renaudiots   B&B €€

(☑ 03 85 86 97 10, mobile 06 16 97 47 80; www.moulinrenaudiots.com; chemin du Vieux Moulin; d €135-165; ⊘ Apr-Oct; ☎⊠) The exterior of this old water mill is 17th-century stately; inside, it's a minimalist's dream, with vast bedrooms, tasteful colour schemes and luxurious linens. The large, gracious garden comes complete with a swimming pool, perfect for an aperitif before enjoying a sumptuous *table d'hôte* meal (€52). The courteous hosts speak excellent English. About 3km from Autun off the road to Châlon-sur-Saône.

Hôtel de la Tête Noire　　　　Hotel €€

(☑03 85 86 59 99; www.hoteltetenoire.fr; 3 rue de l'Arquebuse; s €73-88, d €84-114; ❀🅟) Just a short walk uphill from the tourist office, this well-managed abode is clean, bright and friendly, with a respectable restaurant serving regional dishes on the ground floor. Rooms on the 3rd floor have great views of the town and the countryside.

 Eating

Le Petit Rolin　　　　Crêperie, Burgundian €

(☑03 85 86 15 55; www.le-petit-rolin.fr; place St Louis; crêpes €5-11, menus €13-24; ⊘noon-2pm & 7-9pm daily Apr-Sep, Tue-Sun Oct-Dec, closed Jan-Mar) At Le Petit Rolin, with its rustic interior dating back to the 15th century, the *Bourguignonne galette* is filled with regional ingredients such as Époisses cheese and cured meat. Otherwise there are plenty of fish and meat dishes and salads to choose from. In summer tables fill the square outside, opposite the cathedral's tympanum.

Restaurant Le Chapitre　　　Modern French €€

(☑03 85 52 04 01; www.restaurantlechapitre.com; 11 place du Terreau; mains €15-25, lunch menus €15-20, dinner menus €31-40; ⊘noon-1.30pm Wed-Sun, 7.30pm-9.30pm Tue-Sat) The intimate dining room in brushed-grey tones fills up with locals out for a quiet, elegant meal. Le Chapitre offers a creative French-inspired menu, with a good selection of fish and meat dishes. It's just behind the cathedral.

Le Monde de Don Cabillaud　　　Seafood €€

(☑07 60 94 21 10; 4 rue des Bancs; menus €27-30; ⊘noon-1.30pm & 7-9pm Tue-Sat) This petite restaurant and oyster bar near Musée Rolin might not register high on the stylometer, but the convivial atmosphere makes up for it. The Breton owner serves a small but super-fresh selection of seafood dishes, prepared in a variety of styles and presented with a minimum of fuss.

Le Chalet Bleu　　　Traditional French €€

(☑03 85 86 27 30; www.lechaletbleu.com; 3 rue Jeannin; bistrot menus €19.50-22, restaurant menus €35-60; ⊘noon-2pm Wed-Mon, 7.30pm-9.30pm Wed-Sat) Near the Hôtel de Ville, this place serves classic French gastronomic cuisine in a light,

leafy dining room decorated with colourful frescoes. Options range from attractively priced *bistrot menus* to an eight-course *dégustation menu* featuring gourmet dishes such as foie gras with caramelised pears and walnuts or venison with wild mushrooms. Takeaway plates are also sold next door.

❶ Information

Tourist Office (☑03 85 86 80 38; www.autun-tourisme.com; 13 rue Général Demetz; ⊘9am-12.30pm & 2-6pm Apr-Sep, to 7pm Jul & Aug, closed Sun & Mon Oct-Mar) Sells a self-guided walking-tour brochure (€2) and hiking maps. Has information on the Parc Naturel Régional du Morvan. From June to September, it operates an annexe beside the cathedral.

Tournus

POP 6190

Tournus, on the Saône, is known for its 10th- to 12th-century Romanesque abbey church, **Abbatiale St-Philibert** (⊘8.30am-6pm, to 7pm in summer), whose superb and extremely rare 12th-century mosaic of the calendar and the zodiac was discovered by chance in 2002.

The scenic roads that link Tournus with Cluny, including the D14, D15, D82 and D56, pass through lots of tiny villages, many with charming churches. The medieval hilltop village of **Brancion**, with its 12th-century church and château (adult/child €6/3; ⊘10am-12.30pm & 1-6.30pm), is a lovely place to wander, while **Chardonnay** is, as one would expect, surrounded by vineyards. There's a panoramic view from 579m **Mont St-Romain**.

Cluny

POP 5010

The remains of Cluny's great abbey – Christendom's largest church until the construction of St Peter's Basilica in the Vatican – are fragmentary and scattered, barely discernible among the houses and green spaces of the modern-day town. But with a bit of imagination, it's possible to picture how things looked in the 12th century, when Cluny's Benedictine abbey, renowned for its wealth and power and answerable only to the Pope, held sway over 1100 priories and monasteries stretching from Poland to Portugal.

◉ Sights

Churches of note in the medieval centre include **Église St-Marcel** (rue Prud'hon; ⊘closed to public), topped by an octagonal, three-storey belfry, and **Église Notre Dame** (⊘ 9am-7pm), a 13th-century Gothic church, across from the tourist office.

★ Église Abbatiale
Church

(Abbey Church; ☑ 03 85 59 15 93; www.cluny. monuments-nationaux.fr; combined ticket with Musée d'Art et d'Archéologie adult/child €9.50/free; ⊘ 9.30am-7pm Jul & Aug, to 6pm Apr-Jun & Sep, to 5pm Oct-Mar) Cluny's vast abbey church, built between 1088 and 1130, once extended all the way from the map table in front of the **Palais Jean de Bourbon** to the trees near the octagonal **Clocher de l'Eau Bénite** (Tower of the Holy Water) and the adjoining square **Tour de l'Horloge** (Clock Tower) – a staggering 187m! Virtual reality displays help modern-day visitors envision the grandeur of the medieval abbey while exploring its scant ruins. English-language audioguides and self-guided tour booklets are available.

Abbey visitors also have access to the grounds of the adjacent **École Nationale Supérieure d'Arts et Métiers**, an institute for training mechanical and industrial engineers that's centred on an 18th-century cloister. At the far edge of the grounds, towards the Cluny village exit, don't miss the 13th-century **Farinier** (flour storehouse), under whose soaring wood-framed roof a series of eight finely carved capitals from the abbey's choir are now housed.

Musée d'Art et d'Archéologie
Museum

(combined ticket with Église Abbatiale adult/child €9.50/free; ⊘ 9.30am-7pm Jul & Aug, to 6pm Apr-Jun & Sep, to 5pm Oct-Mar) For an enlightening historical perspective on Cluny and its abbey, start your visit at this archaeological museum inside the Palais Jean de Bourbon. Displays include a model of the Cluny complex, a 10-minute computer-generated 3D 'virtual tour' of the abbey as it looked in the Middle Ages and some superb Romanesque carvings. A combined ticket covers the museum and abbey both.

Tour des Fromages
Tower

(adult/child €2/free; ⊘ 9.30am-12.30pm & 2.30-6pm, no midday closure Jul & Aug, closed Sun Nov-Mar) To better appreciate the abbey's vastness, climb the 120 steps to the top of this tower, once used to ripen cheeses. Access is through the tourist office.

Haras National
Horse Stud

(National Stud Farm; ☑ 03 85 59 85 19; www.haras-nationaux.fr; 2 rue Porte des Prés; adult/child guided tour €6/free, jeudis de Cluny €9/5; ⊘ Feb-Nov)

Founded by Napoléon in 1806, the Haras National houses some of France's finest thoroughbreds, ponies and draught horses. A regular schedule of afternoon guided tours runs from February to November (hours vary by month; see website for details). On Thursdays from mid-July through August, reserve ahead for the 'jeudis de Cluny', special tours that include music and expert riding demonstrations.

🛏 Sleeping

★ Le Clos de l'Abbaye
B&B €

(☑ 03 85 59 22 06; www.closdelabbaye.fr; 6 place du Maré; s €65-75, d €70-75, ste €110-205; 🌐🚗) At this handsome old house directly adjoining the abbey, the four comfortable, colour-coordinated bedrooms – three with abbey views – are flanked by a lovely garden with facilities for kids. Energetic owners Claire and Pascal are excellent tour advisers who direct guests to little-known treasures. There's a wonderful Saturday morning market just outside the front door.

Cluny Séjour
Hostel €

(☑ 03 85 59 08 83; www.cluny-sejour.blogspot. com; 22 rue Porte de Paris; dm/s/d incl breakfast €18/20/37; ⊘ mid-Jan–mid-Dec) Clean, bright two- to four-bed rooms, excellent showers and helpful staff make this simple, well-located hostel a real winner. Towels cost €2.30.

La Pierre Folle
B&B €

(☑ 03 85 59 20 14; www.lapierrefolle.com; incl breakfast s/d/tr/q €70/80/100/120, ste s/d/tr/q €89/102/122/140; 🌐) Surrounded by rolling fields just south of town, this immaculate B&B offers four spacious, comfortable rooms and a single suite. Friendly owners Véronique and Luigi are generous with information about the local area, and serve delicious breakfasts (included) as well as Italian-influenced, four-course *table d'hôte* dinners (€28; book ahead).

Hôtel de Bourgogne
Historic Hotel €€

(☑ 03 85 59 00 58; www.hotel-cluny.com; place de l'Abbaye; d €105-135, ste €135-165; ⊘ Feb-Nov; 🌐) This family-run hotel sits right next to the remains of the abbey. Built in 1817, it has a casual lounge area, 13 antique-furnished rooms and a restaurant. Breakfast is served in an enchanting courtyard. Parking is €10.

Église Abbatiale, Cluny

Eating

The Hôtel de Bourgogne has a fine restaurant.

Le Forum   Italian €

(☑ 03 85 59 31 73; www.leforumcluny.com; Pont de la Levée; pizzas €7-14, mains €10-16; ☺ noon-2pm & 7-10pm Tue-Sat) East across the stream from Cluny's medieval centre, this popular eatery is pleasantly situated in an old stone building with a glassed-in porch and verdant side yard. Specialities include excellent, well-priced pizzas, pasta with creamy truffle sauce, and a good list of French and Italian wines.

Le Bistrot   Bistro €

(☑ 03 85 59 08 07; 14 place du Commerce; mains €9-17; ☺ 8.30am-11pm Wed-Sun; ☎) This character-filled bistro whose walls are adorned with cool vintage posters and old clocks is a real charmer. The flavourful *ravioles* (ravioli with cheese filling) and frondy salads are the house specialities, but there are always imaginative daily specials scrawled on a chalkboard. It doubles as a bar (wine by the glass from €1.20).

★ La Table d'Héloïse   Burgundian €€

(☑ 03 85 59 05 65; www.hostelleriedheloise.com; 7 rte de Mâcon; menus lunch €20, dinner €26-51; ☺ 12.15-1.45pm Fri-Tue, 7.30-8.45pm Mon, Tue & Thu-Sat) Just south of town, this family-run restaurant with a charmingly cosy interior is a terrific place to sample firmly traditional Burgundian specialities, from the dextrously prepared *fricassée d'escargots* (snail stew) to the tender Charolais rumpsteak to the ripe Époisses cheese and the devastatingly delicious homemade desserts. Book ahead for a table in the light-filled verandah overlooking the Grosne River.

Brasserie du Nord   Brasserie €€

(☑ 03 85 59 09 96; place du Maré; mains €10-17, menus €19-32; ☺ 7am-11pm) This brasserie boasts an expansive terrace in a top-notch location – just opposite the Église Abbatiale. The eclectic menu runs the gamut from salads and pasta to frogs' legs and meat dishes. Better still, it's well priced and stays open late (an exception in sedate Cluny).

ℹ Information

Tourist Office (☑ 03 85 59 05 34; www.cluny-tourisme.com; 6 rue Mercière; internet per 15min €1.50; ☺ 9.30am-12.30pm & 2.30-6.30pm, no midday closure Jul & Aug, closed Sun Nov-Mar) Has internet access.

ℹ Getting Around

BICYCLE

Ludisport (☑ 03 85 22 10 62; www.ludisport.com; place des Martyrs de la Déportation; rentals per half/full day from €12/18; ☺ 10am-noon & 2-4pm Apr-Jun & Sep-Nov, 9am-noon & 2-5pm Jul & Aug) rents bicycles at the old train station, about 1km south of the centre.

ROAD TRIP ESSENTIALS

FRANCE DRIVING GUIDE 107

Driving Licence & Documents.........................107
Insurance 107
Hiring a Car 108
Bringing Your Own Vehicle..............................108
Maps 108
Roads & Conditions 109
Road Rules 110
Parking 111
Fuel 112
Satellite Navigation Systems......................... 112
Safety 112
Radio... 112

FRANCE TRAVEL GUIDE........ 113

Getting There & Away 113
Air.. 113
Car & Motorcycle 113
Sea 113
Train.. 113

Directory A–Z.. 114
Accommodation 114
Electricity... 116
Food.. 116
Gay & Lesbian Travellers.................................117
Internet Access 117
Money...117
Opening Hours.. 118
Public Holidays 118
Safe Travel 118
Telephone 119
Toilets...120
Tourist Information...120
Travellers with Disabilities 120
Visas 120

LANGUAGE 121

France Driving Guide

With stunning landscapes, superb highways and one of the world's most scenic and comprehensive secondary road networks, France is a road-tripper's dream come true.

DRIVING LICENCE & DOCUMENTS

Drivers must carry the following at all times:

➡ passport or an EU national ID card

➡ valid driving licence (*permis de conduire*; most foreign licences can be used in France for up to a year)

➡ car-ownership papers, known as a *carte grise* (grey card)

➡ proof of third-party liability *assurance* (insurance)

An International Driving Permit (IDP) is not required when renting a car but can be useful in the event of an accident or police stop, as it translates and vouches for the authenticity of your home licence.

Road Trip Websites

AUTOMOBILE ASSOCIATIONS

RAC (www.rac.co.uk/driving-abroad/france) Info for British drivers on driving in France.

CONDITIONS & TRAFFIC

Bison Futé (www.bison-fute.equipement.gouv.fr)

Les Sociétés d'Autoroutes (www.autoroutes.fr)

ROUTE MAPPING

Mappy (www.mappy.fr)

Via Michelin (www.viamichelin.com)

Driving Fast Facts

Right or left? Drive on the right

Legal driving age 18

Top speed limit 130km/h on *autoroutes* (highways, motorways)

Signature car Citroën 2CV

INSURANCE

Third-party liability insurance *(assurance au tiers)* is compulsory for all vehicles in France, including cars brought from abroad. Normally, cars registered and insured in other European countries can circulate freely. Contact your insurance company before leaving home to make sure you're covered, and to verify whom to call in case of a breakdown or accident.

In a minor accident with no injuries, the easiest way for drivers to sort things out with their insurance companies is to fill out a *Constat Amiable d'Accident Automobile* (accident report), a standardised way of recording important details about what happened. In rental cars it's usually in the packet of documents in the glove compartment. Make sure the report includes any proof that the accident was not your fault. If it *was* your fault you may be liable for a hefty insurance deductible/excess. Don't sign anything you don't fully understand. If necessary, contact the **police** (☑17).

French-registered cars have their insurance-company details printed on a little green square affixed to the windscreen (windshield).

Local Expert: Driving Tips

Driving tips for France from Bert Morris, research consultant for IAM (www.iam. org.uk) and former motoring policy director for the AA:

➡ First thing if you're British: watch your instinct to drive on the left. Once I was leaving a supermarket using the left-turn exit lane. I turned by instinct into the left lane of the street and nearly had a head-on collision. My golden rule: when leaving a parking lot, petrol station or motorway off-ramp, do it on the right and your instinct to stay right will kick in.

➡ French law says to give way to traffic on the right, even when you're on a main road. So I advise people to ease off on the foot whenever you get to a junction.

➡ Never go below a third of a tank, even if you think there's cheaper petrol further down the road; sometimes the next station's a long way off. My approach is, don't fret about cost; you're on holiday!

HIRING A CAR

To hire a car in France, you'll need to be older than 21, with an international credit card. Drivers under 25 usually must pay a surcharge.

All car-hire companies provide mandatory third-party liability insurance, but prices and conditions for collision-damage waiver insurance (CDW, or *assurance tous risques*) vary greatly from company to company. Purchasing the CDW can substantially reduce the *franchise* (deductible/excess) that you'll be liable for if the car is damaged or stolen, but car-hire companies sometimes charge exorbitant rates for this protection; if you travel frequently, sites like www.insurance4carhire. com may provide a cheaper alternative. Your credit card may also cover CDW if you use it to pay for the rental; verify conditions and details with your card issuer.

Arranging your car hire from home is usually considerably cheaper than a walk-in rental, but beware of online offers that don't include CDW or you may be liable for up to 100% of the car's value.

Be sure your car has a spare tyre (it's not uncommon for rentals to be missing these).

International car-hire companies:

Avis (www.avis.com)

Budget (www.budget.com)

Europcar (www.europcar.com)

Hertz (www.hertz.fr)

National-Citer (www.nationalcar.com)

Sixt (www.sixt.com)

French car-hire companies:

ADA (www.ada.fr)

DLM (www.dlm.fr)

France Cars (www.francecars.fr)

Locauto (www.locauto.fr)

Renault Rent (www.renault-rent.com)

Rent a Car Système (www.rentacar.fr)

Internet-based discount brokers:

Auto Europe (www.autoeurope.com)

DriveAway Holidays (driveaway.com.au)

Easycar (www.easycar.com)

Holiday Autos (www.holidayautos.co.uk)

Rental cars with automatic transmission are rare in France; book well ahead for these.

For insurance reasons, rental cars are usually prohibited on ferries, for example to Corsica.

BRINGING YOUR OWN VEHICLE

Any foreign motor vehicle entering France must display a sticker or licence plate identifying its country of registration. Right-hand-drive vehicles brought from the UK or Ireland must have deflectors affixed to the headlights to avoid dazzling oncoming traffic.

MAPS

Michelin's excellent, detailed regional driving maps are highly recommended as a companion to this book, as they will help you navigate back roads and explore alternative routes; IGN's maps are ideal for more specialised activities such as hiking and cycling. Look for both at newsagents, bookshops, airports, supermarkets, tourist offices and service stations along the autoroute.

Institut Géographique National (IGN; www.ign.fr) Publishes regional fold-out maps as well as an all-France volume, *France – Routes, Autoroutes*. Has a great variety of 1:50,000-scale hiking maps, specialised *cyclocartes* (cycling maps) and themed maps showing wine regions, museums etc.

Michelin (boutiquecartesetguides.michelin.fr) Sells excellent, tear-proof yellow-orange 1:200,000-scale regional maps tailor-made for cross-country driving, with precise coverage of smaller back roads.

ROADS & CONDITIONS

France has one of Europe's densest highway networks. There are four types of intercity roads:

Autoroutes (highway names beginning with A) Multilane divided highways, usually with *péage* (tolls). Generously outfitted with rest stops.

Routes Nationales (N, RN) National highways. Some sections have divider strips.

Routes Départementales (D) Local highways and roads.

Routes Communales (C, V) Minor rural roads.

The last two categories, while slower, offer some of France's most enjoyable driving experiences.

Motorcyclists will find France great for touring, with high-quality roads and stunning

Road Distances (KM)

	Bayonne	Bordeaux	Brest	Caen	Cahors	Calais	Chambéry	Cherbourg	Clermont-Ferrand	Dijon	Grenoble	Lille	Lyon	Marseille	Nantes	Nice	Paris	Perpignan	Strasbourg	Toulouse
Bordeaux	184																			
Brest	811	623																		
Caen	764	568	376																	
Cahors	307	218	788	661																
Calais	164	876	710	339	875															
Chambéry	860	651	120	800	523	834														
Cherbourg	835	647	399	124	743	461	923													
Clermont-Ferrand	564	358	805	566	269	717	295	689												
Dijon	807	619	867	548	378	572	273	671	279											
Grenoble	827	657	1126	806	501	863	56	929	300	302										
Lille	997	809	725	353	808	112	767	476	650	505	798									
Lyon	831	528	1018	698	439	755	103	820	171	194	110	687								
Marseille	700	651	1271	1010	521	1067	344	1132	477	506	273	999	314							
Nantes	513	326	298	292	491	593	780	317	462	656	787	609	618	975						
Nice	858	810	1429	1168	679	1225	410	1291	636	664	337	1157	473	190	1131					
Paris	771	583	596	232	582	289	565	355	424	313	571	222	462	775	384	932				
Perpignan	499	451	1070	998	320	1149	478	1094	441	640	445	1081	448	319	773	476	857			
Strasbourg	1254	1066	1079	730	847	621	496	853	584	335	551	522	488	803	867	804	490	935		
Toulouse	300	247	866	865	116	991	565	890	890	727	533	923	536	407	568	564	699	205	1022	
Tours	536	348	490	246	413	531	611	369	369	418	618	463	449	795	197	952	238	795	721	593

scenery. Just make sure your wet-weather gear is up to scratch.

Note that high mountain passes, especially in the Alps, may be closed from as early as September to as late as June. Conditions are posted at the foot of each pass ('*ouvert*' on a green background means open, '*ferme*' on a red background means closed). Snow chains or studded tyres are required in wintry weather.

ROAD RULES

Enforcement of French traffic laws has been stepped up considerably in recent years. Speed cameras are increasingly common, as are radar traps and unmarked police vehicles. Fines for many infractions are given on the spot.

Speed Limits

Speed limits outside built-up areas (unless signposted otherwise):

Undivided N and D highways 90km/h (80km/h when raining)

Non-autoroute divided highways 110km/h (100km/h when raining)

Autoroutes 130km/h (110km/h when raining)

Unless otherwise signposted, a limit of 50km/h applies in *all* areas designated as built up, no matter how rural they may appear. You must slow to 50km/h the moment you come to a town entry sign; this speed limit applies until you pass a town exit sign with a diagonal bar through it.

You're expected to already know the speed limit for various types of roads; that's why most speed-limit signs begin with the word *rappel* (reminder). You can be fined for going as little as 10km over the speed limit.

Alcohol

➡ The blood-alcohol limit is 0.05% (0.5g per litre of blood) – the equivalent of two glasses of wine for a 75kg adult.

➡ Police often conduct random breathalyser tests. Penalties can be severe, including imprisonment.

Motorcycles

➡ Riders of any two-wheeled motorised vehicle must wear a helmet.

➡ No special licence is required to ride a motorbike with an engine smaller than 50cc, which is why rental scooters are often rated at 49.9cc.

➡ As of 1 January 2013, all riders of motorcycles 125cc or larger must wear high-visibility reflective clothing measuring at least 150 sq cm on their upper bodies.

Child Seats

➡ Up to age 10 (or 1.4m tall), children must use a size-appropriate child seat or booster.

➡ Children under 10 cannot ride in the front seat (unless the back is already occupied by other children under 10).

➡ A child under 13kg must travel in a backward-facing child seat.

Other Rules

➡ All passengers, including those in the back seat, must wear seat belts.

➡ Mobile phones may be used only if equipped with a hands-free kit or speakerphone.

➡ Turning right on a red light is illegal.

➡ All vehicles driven in France must carry a high-visibility safety vest, a reflective triangle,

Priority to the Right

Under the *priorité à droite* (priority to the right) rule, any car entering an intersection from a road on your right has the right of way. Don't be surprised if locals courteously cede the right of way when you're about to turn from an alley onto a highway, yet boldly assert their rights when you're the one zipping down a main road.

Priorité à droite is suspended on some main roads marked with a yellow diamond-shaped sign. The same sign with a diagonal bar through it reinstates the *priorité à droite* rule.

At roundabouts where you don't have the right of way (ie the cars already in the roundabout do), you'll see signs reading *vous n'avez pas la priorité* (you do not have right of way) or *cédez le passage* (yield/give way).

Driving Problem-Buster

I can't speak French; will that be a problem? While it's preferable to learn some French before travelling, French road signs are mostly of the 'international symbol' variety, and English is increasingly spoken among the younger generation. Our Language chapter can help you navigate some common roadside emergency situations; in a worst-case scenario, a good attitude and sign language can go a long way.

What should I do if my car breaks down? Safety first: turn on your flashers, put on a safety vest (legally required, and provided in rental-car glove compartments) and place a reflective triangle (also legally required) 30m to 100m behind your car to warn approaching motorists. Call for **emergency assistance** (☑112) or walk to the nearest orange roadside call box (placed every 2km along French *autoroutes*). If renting a vehicle, your car-hire company's service number may help expedite matters. If travelling in your own car, verify before leaving home whether your local auto club has reciprocal roadside-assistance arrangements in France.

What if I have an accident? For minor accidents you'll need to fill out a *Constat Amiable d'Accident* Automobile (accident statement, typically provided in rental-car glove compartments) and report the accident to your insurance and/or rental-car company. If necessary, contact the **police** (☑17).

What should I do if I get stopped by the police? Show your passport (or EU national ID card), licence and proof of insurance. See our Language chapter for some handy phrases.

What's the speed limit in France and how is it enforced? Speed limits (indicated by a black-on-white number inside a red circle) range from 30km/h in small towns to 130km/h on the fastest *autoroutes*. If the motorbike police pull you over, they'll fine you on the spot or direct you to the nearest gendarmerie to pay. If you're caught by a speed camera (placed at random intervals along French highways), the ticket will be sent to your rental-car agency, which will bill your credit card, or to your home address if you're driving your own vehicle. Fines depend on how much you're over the limit.

How do French tolls work? Many French *autoroutes* charge tolls. Take a ticket from the machine upon entering the highway and pay as you exit. Some exit booths are staffed by people; others are automated and will accept only chip-and-PIN credit cards or coins.

What if I can't find anywhere to stay? During summer and holiday periods, book accommodation in advance whenever possible. Local tourist offices can sometimes help find you a bed during normal business hours. Otherwise, try your luck at national chain hotels such as Etap and Formule 1 which are typically clustered at *autoroute* exits outside urban areas.

a spare set of headlight bulbs and (as of 1 July 2012) a portable, single-use breathalyser kit. Noncompliant drivers are subject to fines.

For pictures and descriptions of common French road signs, see the inside back cover.

PARKING

In city centres, most on-the-street parking places are *payant* (metered) from 9am to 7pm Monday to Saturday (sometimes with a midday break). Buy a ticket at the nearest *horodateur* (coin-fed ticket machine) and place it on your dashboard with the time stamp clearly visible. Bigger cities also have public parking garages.

France Playlist

Bonjour Rachid Taha and Gaetan Roussel

Coeur Vagabond Gus Viseur

La Vie en Rose Édith Piaf

Minor Swing Django Reinhardt

L'Americano Akhenaton

Flower Duet from Lakmé Léo Delibes

De Bonnes Raisons Alex Beaupain

FUEL

➡ Diesel (*gazole* or *gasoil*) – €1.35/L; many cars in France run on diesel.

➡ *Essence* (gas/petrol), or *carburant* (fuel) – €1.50/L for 95 unleaded (SP95).

➡ Filling up *(faire le plein)* is most expensive at *autoroute* rest stops, cheapest at hypermarkets.

➡ When renting a car, ask whether it runs on *gazole* or *essence*.

➡ At the pump, diesel nozzles are generally yellow, unleaded gas nozzles green.

➡ Many petrol stations close on Sunday afternoon; even in cities, staffed stations are rarely open late.

➡ After-hours purchases (eg at hypermarkets' fully automatic 24-hour stations) can only be made with a credit card that has an embedded PIN chip. If you don't have a chip-and-PIN card, try to get one from your card company before leaving home; chip-and-PIN cards are also required at many toll booths and train-ticket dispensers throughout France.

SATELLITE NAVIGATION SYSTEMS

Sat-nav devices can be helpful in navigating your way around France. They're commonly available at car-rental agencies, or you can bring your own from home. Accuracy is more dependable on main highways than in small villages or on back roads; in rural areas, don't hesitate to fall back on common sense, road signs and a good Michelin map if your sat nav seems to be leading you astray.

SAFETY

Never leave anything valuable inside your car, even in the boot (trunk). Note that thieves can easily identify rental cars, as they have a distinctive number on the licence plate.

Theft is especially prevalent in the south. In cities like Marseille and Nice, occasional aggressive theft from cars stopped at red lights is also an issue.

RADIO

For news, tune in to the French-language France Info (105.5MHz), the multilanguage RFI (738kHz or 89MHz in Paris) or, in northern France, the BBC World Service (648kHz) and BBC Radio 4 (198kHz). Popular national FM music stations include **NRJ** (www.nrj.fr), **Skyrock** (www.skyrock.fm) and **Nostalgie** (www.nostalgie.fr).

In many areas, Autoroute Info (107.7MHz) has round-the-clock traffic information.

France
Travel Guide

GETTING THERE & AWAY

AIR

International Airports

Rental cars are available at all international airports listed here.

Paris Charles de Gaulle (CDG; www.aeroportsdeparis.fr)

Paris Orly (ORY; www.aeroportsdeparis.fr)

Aéroport de Bordeaux (www.bordeaux.aeroport.fr)

Aéroport de Lille (www.lille.aeroport.fr)

Aéroport Lyon-Saint Exupéry (www.lyonaeroports.com)

EuroAirport (Basel-Mulhouse-Freiburg; www.euroairport.com)

Aéroport Nantes Atlantique (www.nantes.aeroport.fr)

Aéroport Nice Côte d'Azur (societe.nice.aeroport.fr)

Aéroport International Strasbourg (www.strasbourg.aeroport.fr)

Aéroport Toulouse-Blagnac (www.toulouse.aeroport.fr)

CAR & MOTORCYCLE

Entering France from other parts of the EU is usually a breeze – no border checkpoints and no customs – thanks to the Schengen Agreement, signed by all of France's neighbours except the UK, the Channel Islands and Andorra. For these three, old-fashioned document and customs checks are still the norm when exiting France (as well as when entering from Andorra).

Channel Tunnel

The Channel Tunnel (Chunnel), inaugurated in 1994, is the first dry-land link between England and France since the last ice age.

High-speed **Eurotunnel Le Shuttle** (www.eurotunnel.com) trains whisk cars and motorcycles from Folkestone through the Chunnel to Coquelles, 5km southwest of Calais in 35 minutes. Shuttles run 24 hours, with up to three departures an hour during peak time. LPG and CNG tanks are not permitted; gas-powered cars and many campers and caravans have to travel by ferry.

Eurotunnel sets its fares the way budget airlines do: the earlier you book and the lower the demand for a particular crossing, the less you pay; same-day fares can cost a small fortune. Fares for a car, including up to nine passengers, start at £30.

SEA

P&O Ferries (www.poferries.com) and **DFDS Seaways** (www.dfdsseaways.co.uk) both operate regular trans-Channel car ferry service from England to France (primarily from Dover to Calais, with less frequent services from Dover to Dunkirk). **Brittany Ferries** (www.brittanyferries.com) offers additional services from Plymouth, Portsmouth and Poole to the French ports of Roscoff, St-Malo, Cherbourg and Caen.

Ferry companies typically offer discounts for advance booking and/or off-peak travel. Seasonal demand is a crucial factor (Christmas, Easter, UK and French school holidays, July and August are especially busy), as is the time of day (an early-evening ferry can cost much more than one at 4am).

For the best fares, check **Ferry Savers** (www.ferrysavers.com).

TRAIN

Rail services link France with virtually every country in Europe. The **Eurostar** (www.eurostar.com) whisks passengers from London to Paris in 2¼ hours.

You can book tickets and get train information from **Rail Europe** (www.raileurope.com). In France ticketing is handled by the national railway company **SNCF** (www.sncf.com). High-speed train travel between France and the UK, Belgium, the Netherlands, Germany and Austria is covered by **Railteam** (www.railteam.co.uk) and **TGV-Europe** (www.tgv-europe.com).

Avis (www.avis.fr), in partnership with **SNCF** (www.voyages-sncf.com/train/train-avis), has rental-car agencies in most major French railway stations. Cars booked through the SNCF website may be picked up from an SNCF representative after hours if the Avis office is closed.

DIRECTORY A–Z

ACCOMMODATION

Be it a fairy-tale château, a boutique hideaway or floating pod on a lake, France has accommodation to suit every taste, mood and pocket.

Categories

Budget covers everything from hostels to small, simple family-run places; midrange means a few extra creature comforts such as satellite TV and free wi-fi; and top-end places stretch from luxury five-star palaces with air conditioning, pools and restaurants to boutique-chic chalets in the Alps.

Costs

Accommodation costs vary wildly between seasons and regions: what will buy you a night in a romantic *chambre d'hôte* (B&B) in the countryside may only get you a dorm bed in a major city or high-profile ski resort.

Reservations

Midrange, top-end and many budget hotels require a credit card to secure a reservation. Tourist offices can often advise on availability and reserve for you, sometimes charging a small fee.

Seasons

➡ In ski resorts, high season is Christmas, New Year and the February–March school holidays.

➡ On the coast, high season is summer, particularly August.

➡ Hotels in inland cities often charge low-season rates in summer.

➡ Rates often drop outside the high season – in some cases by as much as 50%.

➡ In business-oriented hotels in cities, rooms are most expensive from Monday to Thursday and cheaper over the weekend.

➡ In the Alps, hotels usually close between seasons, from around May to mid-June and from mid-September to early December; many addresses in Corsica only open April to October.

B&Bs

For charm, it's hard to beat privately run *chambres d'hôte* (B&Bs), available throughout rural France. By law a *chambre d'hôte must* have no more than five rooms and breakfast must be included in the price; some hosts prepare home-cooked evening meals *(table d'hôte)* for an extra charge of €20 to €30. Pick up lists of *chambres d'hôte* at local tourist offices, or consult the following websites:

Bienvenue à la Ferme (www.bienvenue-a-la-ferme.com) Farmstays.

Chambres d'hôtes de Charme (www.guidesdecharme.com) Boutique B&Bs.

Chambres d'Hôtes France (www.chambresdhotesfrance.com)

en France (www.bbfrance.com) B&Bs and *gîtes* (self-catering cottages).

Fleurs de Soleil (www.fleursdesoleil.fr) Stylish *maisons d'hôte,* mainly in rural France.

Gîtes de France (www.gites-de-france.com) France's primary umbrella organisation for B&Bs and *gîtes*. Search for properties by region, theme (with kids, by the sea, gourmet, etc) or activity (fishing, wine tasting etc) or facilities (pool, dishwasher, fireplace, baby equipment etc).

Practicalities

Time France uses the 24-hour clock and is on Central European Time, which is one hour ahead of GMT/UTC. During daylight-saving time, from the last Sunday in March to the last Sunday in October, France is two hours ahead of GMT/UTC.

TV & DVD TV is Secam; DVDs are zone 2; videos work on the PAL system.

Weights & Measures France uses the metric system.

Sleeping Price Ranges

The following price ranges refer to a double room with private bathroom in high season (breakfast is not included, except at B&Bs).

€	less than €80
€€	€80–180
€€€	more than €180

Guides de Charme (www.guidesdecharme. com) Upmarket B&Bs.

Samedi Midi Éditions (www.samedimidi. com) *Chambres d'hôte* organised by location or theme.

Camping

Camping is extremely popular in France. There are thousands of well-equipped campgrounds, many considerably placed by rivers, lakes and the sea. Gîtes de France and Bienvenue à la Ferme coordinate camping on farms.

➡ Most campgrounds open March or April to late September or October; popular spots fill up fast in summer, when it's wise to book ahead.

➡ Economisers should look out for local, good-value but no-frills *campings municipaux* (municipal campgrounds).

➡ Many campgrounds rent mobile homes with mod cons like heating, kitchen and TV.

➡ Camping 'wild' in nondesignated spots (*camping sauvage*) is illegal in France.

➡ Campsite offices often close during the day.

Websites with campsite listings searchable by location, theme and facilities:

Camping en France (www.camping.fr)

Camping France (www.campingfrance.com)

Guide du Camping (www.guideducamp ing.com)

HPA Guide (http://camping.hpaguide.com)

Hostels

Hostels in France range from spartan rooms to hip hang-outs with perks aplenty.

➡ In university towns, *foyers d'étudiant* (student dormitories) are sometimes converted for use by travellers during summer.

➡ A dorm bed in an *auberge de jeunesse* (youth hostel) costs from €10.50 to €28 depending on location, amenities and facilities; sheets are always included, breakfast more often than not.

➡ Hostels by the sea or in the mountains sometimes offer seasonal outdoor activities.

➡ French hostels are 100% nonsmoking.

Hotels

We have tried to feature well-situated, independent hotels that offer good value, a warm welcome, at least a bit of charm and a palpable sense of place.

➡ Hotels in France are rated with one to five stars, although the ratings are based on highly objective criteria (eg the size of the entry hall), not the quality of the service, the decor or cleanliness.

➡ French hotels rarely include breakfast in their rates. Unless specified otherwise, prices quoted don't include breakfast, which costs around €7/10/20 in a budget/midrange/top-end hotel.

➡ A double room generally has one double bed (sometimes two singles pushed together!); a room with twin beds *(deux lits)* is usually more expensive, as is a room with a bathtub instead of a shower.

➡ Feather pillows are practically nonexistent in France, even in top-end hotels.

➡ All hotel restaurant terraces allow smoking; if you are sensitive to smoke sit inside or carry a respirator.

Chain Hotels

Chain hotels stretch from nondescript establishments near the *autoroute* (motorway, highway) to central four-star hotels with character. Most conform to certain standards of decor, service and facilities (air-conditioning, free wi-fi, 24-hour check-in etc), and offer competitive rates as well as last-minute, weekend and/or online deals.

Book Your Stay Online

For more accommodation reviews by Lonely Planet authors, check out http://hotels.lonelyplanet.com. You'll find independent reviews, as well as recommendations on the best places to stay. Best of all, you can book online.

Countrywide biggies:

B&B Hôtels (www.hotel-bb.com) Cheap motel-style digs.

Best Western (www.bestwestern.com) Independent two- to four-star hotels, each with its own local character.

Campanile (www.campanile.com) Good-value hotels geared up for families.

Citôtel (www.citotel.com) Independent two- and three-star hotels.

Contact Hôtel (www.contact-hotel.com) Inexpensive two- and three-star hotels.

Etap (www.etaphotel.com) Ubiquitous chain.

Formule 1 (www.hotelformule1.com) Non-descript roadside cheapie.

Ibis (www.ibishotel.com) Midrange pick.

Inter-Hotel (www.inter-hotel.fr) Two- and three-star hotels, some quite charming.

Kyriad (www.kyriad.com) Comfortable midrange choices.

Novotel (www.novotel.com) Family-friendly.

Première Classe (www.premiereclasse.com) Motel-style accommodation.

Sofitel (www.sofitel.com) Range of top-end hotels in major French cities.

ELECTRICITY

European two-pin plugs are standard. France has 230V at 50Hz AC (you may need a transformer for 110V electrical appliances).

230V/50Hz

FOOD

Food-happy France has a seemingly endless variety of eateries; categories listed here are found throughout the country: The Eating & Sleeping sections of this guide include phone numbers for places that require reservations (typically higher-end bistros or family-run enterprises such as *tables d'hôte*).

Auberge Country inn serving traditional fare, often attached to a B&B or small hotel.

Ferme auberge Working farm that cooks up meals – only dinner usually – from local farm products.

Bistro (also spelt *bistrot*) Anything from a pub or bar with snacks and light meals to a small, fully fledged restaurant.

Brasserie Much like a cafe except it serves full meals, drinks and coffee from morning until 11pm or later. Typical fare includes *choucroute* (sauerkraut) and *moules frites* (mussels and fries).

Restaurant Born in Paris in the 18th century, restaurants today serve lunch and dinner five or six days a week.

Cafe Basic light snacks as well as drinks.

Crêperie (also *galetterie*) Casual address specialising in sweet crêpes and savoury *galettes* (buckwheat crêpes).

Salon de Thé Trendy tearoom often serving light lunches (quiche, salads, cakes, tarts, pies and pastries) as well as black and herbal teas.

Table d'hôte (literally 'host's table') Some of the most charming B&Bs serve *table d'hôte*, a delicious homemade meal of set courses with little or no choice.

Eating Price Ranges

The following price ranges refer to a two-course set menu (ie entrée plus main course or main course plus dessert), with tax and service charge included in the price.

€	less than €20
€€	€20–40
€€€	more than €40

GAY & LESBIAN TRAVELLERS

The rainbow flag flies high in France, a country that left its closet long before many of its European neighbours. *Laissez-faire* perfectly sums up France's liberal attitude towards homosexuality and people's private lives in general. Paris, Bordeaux, Lille, Lyon, Montpellier and Toulouse are among the many cities with thriving gay and lesbian scenes. Attitudes towards homosexuality tend to be more conservative in the countryside and villages. France's lesbian scene is less public than its gay male counterpart.

Publications

Damron (www.damron.com) Publishes English-language travel guides, including the *Damron Women's Traveller* for lesbians and the *Damron Men's Travel Guide* for gays.

Spartacus International Gay Guide (www.spartacusworld.com) A male-only guide with more than 70 pages devoted to France, almost half of which cover Paris. iPhone app too.

Websites

France Queer Resources Directory (www.france.qrd.org) Gay and lesbian directory.

French Government Tourist Office (www.us.franceguide.com/special-interests/gay-friendly) Information about 'the gay-friendly destination par excellence'.

Gay France (www.gay-france.net) Insider tips on gay life in France.

Gayscape (www.gayscape.com) Hundreds of links to gay- and lesbian-related sites.

Gayvox (www.gayvox.com/guide3) Online travel guide to France, with listings by region.

Tasse de Thé (www.tassedethe.com) A *webzine lesbien* with lots of useful links.

INTERNET ACCESS

➡ Wireless (wi-fi) access points can be found at major airports, in many hotels and at some cafes.

➡ Some tourist offices and numerous cafes and bars tout wi-fi hot spots that let laptop owners hook up for free.

➡ To search for free wi-fi hot spots in France, visit www.hotspot-locations.co.uk or www.free-hotspot.com.

➡ Internet cafes are becoming less rife, but at least one can still be found in most large towns and cities. Prices range from €2 to €6 per hour.

➡ If accessing dial-up ISPs with your laptop, you'll need a telephone-plug adaptor, available at large supermarkets.

MONEY

ATMs

Known as *distributeurs automatiques de billets* (DAB) or *points d'argent* in French, ATMs are the cheapest and most convenient way to get money. Those connected to international networks are ubiquitous and usually offer an excellent exchange rate.

Cash

You always get a better exchange rate in-country, but if arriving in France by air or late at night, you may want to bring enough euros to take a taxi to a hotel.

Credit & Debit Cards

➡ Credit and debit cards, accepted almost everywhere in France, are convenient and relatively secure and usually offer a better exchange rate than travellers cheques or cash exchanges.

➡ Credit cards issued in France have embedded chips – you have to type in a PIN to make a purchase.

➡ Visa, MasterCard and Amex can be used in shops and supermarkets and for train travel, car hire and motorway tolls, though some places (eg 24-hour petrol stations, some autoroute toll machines) only take French-style credit cards with chips and PINs.

➡ Don't assume that you can pay for a meal or a budget hotel with a credit card – enquire first.

➡ Cash advances are a supremely convenient way to stay stocked up with euros, but getting cash with a credit card involves both fees (sometimes US$10 or more) and interest – ask your credit-card issuer for details. Debit-card fees are usually much less.

Moneychangers

➡ In Paris and major cities, *bureaux de change* (exchange bureaus) are open longer hours, give faster and easier service and often have better rates than banks.

➡ Some post-office branches exchange travellers cheques and banknotes; most won't take US$100 bills.

Tipping Guide

By law, restaurant and bar prices are *service compris* (include a 15% service charge), so there is no need to leave a *pourboire* (tip). If you were extremely satisfied with the service, however, you can – as many locals do – leave a small 'extra' tip for your waiter or waitress.

bars	round to nearest euro
hotel cleaning staff	€1-1.50 per day
hotel porters	€1-1.50 per bag
restaurants	5-10%
taxis	10-15%
toilet attendants	€0.20-0.50
tour guides	€1-2 per person

OPENING HOURS

Below are standard hours for various types of business in France (note that these can fluctuate by an hour either way in some cases). For individual business listings in this book, we've only included opening hours where they differ significantly from these standards:

banks	9am-noon & 2-5pm Mon-Fri or Tue-Sat
bars	7pm-1am Mon-Sat
cafes	7am or 8am-10pm or 11pm Mon-Sat
nightclubs	10pm-3am, 4am or 5am Thu-Sat
post offices	8.30am or 9am-5pm or 6pm Mon-Fri, 8am-noon Sat
restaurants	lunch noon-2.30pm, dinner 7-11pm six days a week
shops	9am or 10am-7pm Mon-Sat (often with lunch break noon-1.30pm)
supermarkets	8.30am-7pm Mon-Sat, 8.30am-12.30pm Sun

PUBLIC HOLIDAYS

The following *jours fériés* (public holidays) are observed in France:

New Year's Day (Jour de l'An) 1 January.

Easter Sunday and Monday (Pâques and lundi de Pâques) Late March/April.

May Day (Fête du Travail) 1 May.

Victoire 1945 8 May – commemorates the Allied victory in Europe that ended WWII.

Ascension Thursday (Ascension) May – celebrated on the 40th day after Easter.

Pentecost/Whit Sunday and Whit Monday (Pentecôte and lundi de Pentecôte) Mid-May to mid-June – celebrated on the seventh Sunday after Easter.

Bastille Day/National Day (Fête Nationale) 14 July – *the* national holiday.

Assumption Day (Assomption) 15 August.

All Saints' Day (Toussaint) 1 November.

Remembrance Day (L'onze novembre) 11 November – marks the WWI armistice.

Christmas (Noël) 25 December.

SAFE TRAVEL

France is generally a safe place to travel, though crime has risen substantially in recent years. Property crime is much more common than physical violence; it's extremely unlikely that you will be assaulted while walking down the street. Always check your government's travel advisory warnings.

Hunting is traditional and commonplace throughout rural France, and the season runs from September to February. If you see signs reading 'chasseurs' or 'chasse gardée' strung up or tacked to trees, think twice about wandering into the area.

Natural Dangers

➡ There are powerful tides and strong undertows at many places along the Atlantic coast, from the Spanish border north to Brittany and Normandy.

➡ Only swim in zones de baignade surveillée (beaches monitored by life guards).

➡ Be aware of tide times and the high-tide mark if walking on a beach.

➡ Thunderstorms in the mountains and the hot southern plains can be extremely sudden and violent.

➡ Check the weather report before setting out on a long walk and be prepared for sudden temperature drops if you're heading into the high country of the Alps or Pyrenees.

➡ Avalanches pose a significant danger in the Alps.

Theft

There's no need to travel in fear, but it is worth taking a few simple precautions against theft.

➡ Break-ins to parked cars are not uncommon. Never leave anything valuable inside your car, even in the boot (trunk).

➡ Aggressive theft from cars stopped at red lights is occasionally a problem, especially in Marseille and Nice. As a precaution, lock your car doors and roll up the windows in major urban areas.

➡ Pickpocketing and bag snatching (eg in dense crowds and public places) are prevalent in big cities, particularly Paris, Marseille and Nice. Be especially vigilant for bag-snatchers at outdoor cafes and beaches.

- - - - - - - - - - - - - - - - - - -

TELEPHONE

Mobile Phones

➡ French mobile-phone numbers begin with ☎06 or ☎07.

➡ France uses GSM 900/1800, which is compatible with the rest of Europe and Australia but not with the North American GSM 1900 or the totally different system in Japan (though some North Americans have tri-band phones that work in France).

➡ Check with your service provider about roaming charges – dialling a mobile phone from a fixed-line phone or another mobile can be incredibly expensive.

➡ It may be cheaper to buy your own French SIM card – and locals you meet are much more likely to ring you if your number is French.

➡ If you already have a compatible phone, you can slip in a SIM card (€20 to €30) and rev it up with prepaid credit, though this is likely to run out fast as domestic prepaid calls cost about €0.50 per minute.

➡ Recharge cards are sold at most tabacs and newsagents.

➡ SIMs are available at the ubiquitous outlets run by France's three mobile-phone companies, **Bouygues** (www.bouyguestelecom.fr), **Orange** (www.orange.com) and **SFR** (www.sfr.com).

Phone Codes

Calling France from abroad Dial your country's international access code, then ☎33 (France's country code), then the 10-digit local number *without* the initial zero.

Calling internationally from France Dial ☎00 (the international access code), the *indicatif* (country code), the area code (without the initial zero if there is one) and the local number. Some country codes are posted in public telephones.

Directory enquiries For national *service des renseignements* (directory enquiries) dial ☎11 87 12 (€1.46 per call, plus €0.45 per minute), or use the service for free online at www.118712.fr.

Emergency numbers Can be dialled from public phones without a phonecard.

Hotel calls Hotels, *gîtes,* hostels and *chambres d'hôte* are free to meter their calls as they like. The surcharge is usually around €0.30 per minute but can be higher.

International directory enquiries For numbers outside France, dial ☎11 87 00 (€2 to €3 per call).

Phonecards

➡ For explanations in English and other languages on how to use a public telephone, push the button engraved with a two-flags icon.

➡ For both international and domestic calling, most public phones operate using either a credit card or two kinds of *télécartes* (phonecards): *cartes à puce* (cards with a magnetic chip) issued by Orange (formerly France Télécom) and sold at post offices for €8 or €15; and *cartes à code* (cards where you dial a free access number and then the card's scratch-off code), sold at *tabacs*, newsagents and post offices.

➡ Phonecards with codes offer *much* better international rates than Orange chip cards or Country Direct services (for which you are billed at home by your long-distance carrier).

➡ The shop you buy a phonecard from should be able to tell you which type is best for the country you want to call. Using phonecards from a home phone is much cheaper that using them from public phones or mobile phones.

TOILETS

Public toilets around France are signposted WC or *toilettes*. These range from spiffy 24-hour mechanical self-cleaning toilets costing around €0.50 to hole-in-the-floor *toilettes à la turque* (squat toilets) at older establishments and motorway stops. In the most basic places you may need to supply your own paper.

The French are more blasé about unisex toilets than elsewhere, so save your blushes when tiptoeing past the urinals to reach the ladies' loo.

TOURIST INFORMATION

Almost every city, town, village and hamlet has a clearly signposted *office de tourisme* (government-run tourist office) or *syndicat d'initiative* (tourist office run by local merchants). Both can supply you with local maps as well as details on accommodation, restaurants and activities such as walking, cycling or wine tasting. Useful websites:

French Government Tourist Office (www.franceguide.com) The low-down on sights, activities, transport and special-interest holidays in all of France's regions. Brochures can be downloaded online. There are links to country-specific websites.

Réseau National des Destinations Départementales (www.fncdt.net) Listing of CRT (regional tourist board) websites.

TRAVELLERS WITH DISABILITIES

While France presents evident challenges for *handicapés* (people with disabilities) – namely cobblestone, cafe-lined streets that are a nightmare to navigate in a wheelchair, a lack of curb ramps, older public facilities and many budget hotels without lifts – you can still enjoy travelling here with a little careful planning.

Whether you are looking for wheelchair-friendly accommodation, sights, attractions or restaurants, these associations and agencies can help:

Association des Paralysés de France (APF; www.apf.asso.fr) National organisation for people with disabilities, with offices throughout France.

Tourisme et Handicaps (www.tourisme-handicaps.org) Issues the 'Tourisme et Handicap' label to tourist sites, restaurants and hotels that comply with strict accessibility and usability standards. Different symbols indicate the sort of access afforded to people with physical, mental, hearing and/or visual disabilities.

VISAS

For up-to-date details on visa requirements, see the website of the **Ministère des Affaires Étrangères** (Ministry of Foreign Affairs; www.diplomatie.gouv.fr/en) and click 'Coming to France'. Visas are not required for EU nationals or citizens of Iceland, Norway and Switzerland, and are required only for stays greater than 90 days for citizens of Australia, the USA, Canada, Hong Kong, Israel, Japan, Malaysia, New Zealand, Singapore, South Korea and many Latin American countries.

Language

The sounds used in spoken French can almost all be found in English. There are a couple of exceptions: nasal vowels (represented in our pronunciation guides by o or u followed by an almost inaudible nasal consonant sound m, n or ng), the 'funny' *u* (ew in our guides) and the deep-in-the-throat *r*. Bearing these few points in mind and reading our pronunciation guides below as if they were English, you'll be understood just fine.

BASICS

Hello.	*Bonjour.*	bon·zhoor
Goodbye.	*Au revoir.*	o·rer·vwa
Yes./No.	*Oui./Non.*	wee/non
Excuse me.	*Excusez-moi.*	ek·skew·zay·mwa
Sorry.	*Pardon.*	par·don
Please.	*S'il vous plaît.*	seel voo play
Thank you.	*Merci.*	mair·see

You're welcome.
De rien. der ree·en

Do you speak English?
Parlez-vous anglais? par·lay·voo ong·glay

I don't understand.
Je ne comprends pas. zher ner kom·pron pa

How much is this?
C'est combien? say kom·byun

ACCOMMODATION

Do you have any rooms available?
Est-ce que vous avez es·ker voo za·vay
des chambres libres? day shom·brer lee·brer

How much is it per night/person?
Quel est le prix kel ay ler pree
par nuit/personne? par nwee/per·son

DIRECTIONS

Can you show me (on the map)?
Pouvez-vous m'indiquer poo·vay·voo mun·dee·kay
(sur la carte)? (sewr la kart)

Where's ...?
Où est ...? oo ay ...

EATING & DRINKING

What would you recommend?
Qu'est-ce que vous kes·ker voo
conseillez? kon·say·yay

I'd like ..., please.
Je voudrais ..., zher voo·dray ...
s'il vous plaît. seel voo play

I'm a vegetarian.
Je suis végétarien/ zher swee vay·zhay·ta·ryun/
végétarienne. vay·zhay·ta·ryen (m/f)

Please bring the bill.
Apportez-moi a·por·tay·mwa
l'addition, la·dee·syon
s'il vous plaît. seel voo play

EMERGENCIES

Help!
Au secours! o skoor

I'm lost.
Je suis perdu/perdue. zhe swee·pair·dew (m/f)

I'm ill.
Je suis malade. zher swee ma·lad

Want More?

For in-depth language information and handy phrases, check out Lonely Planet's *French Phrasebook*. You'll find it at **shop.lonelyplanet.com**, or you can buy Lonely Planet's iPhone phrasebooks at the Apple App Store.

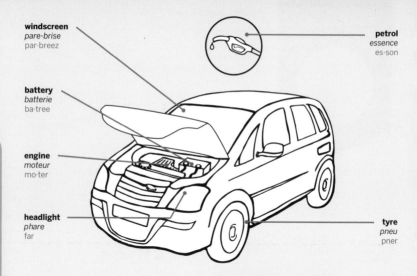

windscreen
pare-brise
par·breez

petrol
essence
es·son

battery
batterie
ba·tree

engine
moteur
mo·ter

headlight
phare
far

tyre
pneu
pner

Signs

Cédez la Priorité	Give Way
Sens Interdit	No Entry
Entrée	Entrance
Péage	Toll
Sens Unique	One Way
Sortie	Exit

Call the police!
Appelez la police!   a·play la po·lees

Call a doctor!
Appelez un médecin!   a·play un mayd·sun

ON THE ROAD

I'd like to hire a/an ...	*Je voudrais louer ...*	zher voo·dray loo·way ...
4WD	*un quatre-quatre*	un kat·kat
automatic/ manual	*une automatique/ manuel*	ewn o·to·ma·teek/ ma·nwel
motorbike	*une moto*	ewn mo·to

How much is it daily/weekly?
Quel est le tarif par jour/semaine?   kel ay ler ta·reef par zhoor/ser·men

Does that include insurance?
Est-ce que l'assurance est comprise?   es·ker la·sew·rons ay kom·preez

Does that include mileage?
Est-ce que le kilométrage est compris?   es·ker ler kee·lo·may·trazh ay kom·pree

What's the speed limit?
Quelle est la vitesse maximale permise?   kel ay la vee·tes mak·see·mal per·meez

Is this the road to ...?
C'est la route pour ...?   say la root poor ...

Can I park here?
Est-ce que je peux stationner ici?   es·ker zher per sta·syo·nay ee·see

Where's a service station?
Où est-ce qu'il y a une station-service?   oo es·keel ya ewn sta·syon·ser·vees

Please fill it up.
Le plein, s'il vous plaît.   ler plun seel voo play

I'd like (20) litres.
Je voudrais (vingt) litres.   zher voo·dray (vung) lee·trer

Please check the oil/water.
Contrôlez l'huile/l'eau, s'il vous plaît.   kon·tro·lay lweel/lo seel voo play

I need a mechanic.
J'ai besoin d'un mécanicien.   zhay ber·zwun dun may·ka·nee·syun

The car/motorbike has broken down.
La voiture/moto est tombée en panne.   la vwa·tewr/mo·to ay tom·bay on pan

I had an accident.
J'ai eu un accident.   zhay ew un ak·see·don

BEHIND THE SCENES

SEND US YOUR FEEDBACK

We love to hear from travellers – your comments help make our books better. We read every word, and we guarantee that your feedback goes straight to the authors. Visit **lonelyplanet. com/contact** to submit your updates and suggestions.

Note: We may edit, reproduce and incorporate your comments in Lonely Planet products such as guidebooks, websites and digital products, so let us know if you don't want your comments reproduced or your name acknowledged. For a copy of our privacy policy visit lonelyplanet.com/privacy.

ACKNOWLEDGMENTS

Climate map data adapted from Peel MC, Finlayson BL & McMahon TA (2007) 'Updated World Map of the Köppen-Geiger Climate Classification', *Hydrology and Earth System Sciences*, 11, 163344.

Cover photographs: (front) Château de Chenonceau, David A Barnes/Alamy; (back) Château de Chambord, Viacheslav Lopatin/Shutterstock

THIS BOOK

This 1st edition of *Châteaux of the Loire Valley Road Trips* was researched and written by Alexis Averbuck, Oliver Berry, Jean-Bernard Carillet and Gregor Clark. This guidebook was produced by the following:

Product Editor Anne Mason

Senior Cartographer Valentina Kremenchutskaya

Book Designer Katherine Marsh

Assisting Editor Melanie Dankel

Cover Researcher Brendan Dempsey

Thanks to Shahara Ahmed, Sasha Baskett, James Hardy, Campbell McKenzie, Darren O'Connell, Angela Tinson, Tony Wheeler

OUR STORY

A beat-up old car, a few dollars in the pocket and a sense of adventure. In 1972 that's all Tony and Maureen Wheeler needed for the trip of a lifetime – across Europe and Asia overland to Australia. It took several months, and at the end – broke but inspired – they sat at their kitchen table writing and stapling together their first travel guide, *Across Asia on the Cheap*. Within a week they'd sold 1500 copies. Lonely Planet was born.

Today, Lonely Planet has offices in Melbourne, London and Oakland, with more than 600 staff and writers. We share Tony's belief that 'a great guidebook should do three things: inform, educate and amuse'.

INDEX

A

Abbaye de Fontenay 44-5
Abbaye de Fontevraud 32, 83-4
accommodation 15, 114, *see also individual locations*
air travel 15, 113
Aloxe-Corton 49-50
Amboise 23-5, 72-4
Angers 35, 85-8, **86**
Anjou 79-88
area codes 119-20
art, *see* museums & galleries
ATMs 117
Autun 42-3, 101-3
Azay-le-Rideau 22, 76-7

B

Basilique St-Martin 69
bathrooms 120
Beaune 42, 50, 93-7, **94**
Blésois 61-87
Blois 25-6, 61-4
boat travel 113
border crossings 113
bureaux de change 117-19
Burgundy 39-45, 47-53, 89-105, **6-7**, **40-1**
business hours 118

C

Candes-St-Martin 32, 83
car hire 14, 108
car insurance 107
car travel, *see* driving
cash 117
cassis 90
cathedrals, *see* churches & cathedrals
caves 29-35, 36, 74, 84
Caves Monmousseau 74
Caves Painctes de Chinon 36
cell phones 15
châteaux
    Château d'Angers 35, 85-6
    Château d'Azay-le-Rideau 22, 76-7
    Château de Beauregard 67-8
    Château de Brézé 34, 84-5
    Château de Brissac 34-5, 88
    Château de Chambord 24, 26, 65-6
    Château de Chaumont-sur-Loire 66-7
    Château de Chenonceau 22-3, 71-2
    Château de Cheverny 26, 66-7
    Château de La Rochepot 52-3, 92
    Château de Langeais 21-2, 75-6

Château de Meursault 50-2, 92
Château de Montsoreau 32, 83
Château de Pommard 50, 92
Château de Saumur 31, 80
Château de Savigny 92
Château de Serrant 88
Château de Villandry 22, 75
Château du Clos de Vougeot 49, 90
Château d'Ussé 77-8
Château Royal d'Amboise 72
Château Royal de Blois 25-6, 62-3
discount tickets 65, 77
Loire Valley 19-27
children, travel with 60
Chinon 21, 33, 36-7, 77-9, **37**
churches & cathedrals
    Basilique Collégiale Notre Dame 95
    Basilique Ste-Madeleine 99
    Basilique St-Martin 69
    Cathédrale Ste-Croix 58
    Cathédrale St-Gatien 69
    Cathédrale St-Lazare 102
    Chapelle Ste-Radegonde 37
    Église Abbatiale 104
Cité Royale 23
climate 14
Cluny 40-1, 103-5
costs 15, 114, 115, 116

000 Map pages

Côte de Beaune 92-3
Côte de Nuits 89-91
credit cards 117
currency 14

D

da Vinci, Leonardo 73
dangers 109-10, 111, 112, 118-19
debit cards 117
Dijon 42
disabilities, travellers with 120
distilleries
  absinthe 80
  cassis 90
  Triple Sec 80
Domaine National de Chambord 65
Doué-la-Fontaine 34
driving 107-12, 113
  car hire 14, 108
  fuel 14
  insurance 107
  licences 107
  maps 108-9
  music 112
  parking 111
  road distances 109
  road rules 110-11
  safety 109-10, 111, 112
  satellite navigation systems 112
  speed limits 111
  tolls 111
  websites 15, 107
DVDs 114

E

École Nationale d'Équitation 31
Église Abbatiale 104
electricity 116
emergencies 14
escargots 50

F

Fontevraud-l'Abbaye 83-4
food 11, 15, see also individual locations
Forteresse Royale de Chinon 37
François I 65
French language 121-2
fuel 14

G

gas 14
gay travellers 117
Gevrey-Chambertin 49
GPS 112

H

holidays 118
Hostellerie Gargantua 36

I

insurance 107
internet access 15

J

Jeanne d'Arc 57-8

L

La Cave Voltaire 37
La Devinière 33-4
language 121-2
Le Clos Lucé 73
lesbian travellers 117
Loches 23
Loire Valley 19-27, 29-35, 56-88, **6-7**

M

maps 108-9
measures 114
mobile phones 15
money 14, 15, 115, 116, 117-19

Montsoreau 32, 83
motorcycles, see driving
museums & galleries
  CERCIL 60
  Fondation du Doute 63
  Galerie David d'Angers 85
  L'Imaginarium 49, 90
  Maison de Jeanne d'Arc 59-60
  Maison de la Magie 63
  Musée Balzac 78
  Musée d'Art et d'Archéologie 104
  Musée d'Art et d'Histoire 36
  Musée de la Cavalerie 80
  Musée des Beaux-Arts (Angers) 85
  Musée des Beaux-Arts (Orléans) 59
  Musée des Beaux-Arts (Tours) 67
  Musée des Blindés 80
  Musée du Compagnonnage 69
  Musée Historique et Archéologique 59-60
  Musée Jean Lurçat et de la Tapisserie Contemporaine 85
  Musée Rabelais 33-4
  Musée Rolin 102
  Musée Zervos 99
music 112
mustard 94-5

N

navigation systems 112
Noyers-sur-Serein 45, 98-9
Nuits-St-Georges 49, 89-90

O

opening hours 118
Orléanais 57-61
Orléans 57-61, **58**

P

Palais des Ducs et des
  États de Bourgogne 42
Parc Naturel Régional
  du Morvan 43
Paris 10-11, 12-13, **13**
parking 11, 111
petrol 14
phonecards 120
public holidays 118
Puligny-Montrachet 53, 90-1

R

radio 112
road distances 109
road rules 108, 110-11
Rochemenier 34, 84
Route des Grands Crus
  47-53

S

safety 109-10, 111, 112, 118-19
satellite navigation
  systems 112
Saumur 31, 79-83
Semur-en-Auxois 43-4
speed limits 111

St-Hilaire-St-Florent 35
St-Romain 52

T

telephone services 15
theft 119
time 114
tipping 15, 118
toilets 120
tolls 111
Touraine 67-88
tourist information 120
Tournus 41-2, 103
Tours 67-71, **68**
train travel 113-14
transport 11, 15, *see also*
  driving
troglodytes 84
Troglodytes et
  Sarcophages 34
Turquant 31-2, 82-3
TV 114

V

vacations 118
Vézelay 45
Villandry 22, 75
visas 14

W

walking tours
  Chinon 36-7, **37**
  Paris 12-13, **13**
weather 14
websites 11, 15
weights 114
wifi 15
wine
  Burgundy 52
  Loire Valley 62, 82
wine routes
  Côte de Beaune 92-3
  Côte de Nuits 89-91
  Route des Grands Crus
    47-53
wineries
  Caves Monmousseau 74
  Château de Meursault 92
  Château de Pommard 92
  Château de Savigny 92
  Château du Clos de
    Vougeot 90
  Loire Valley 82
  Turquant 82-3

000 Map pages

Jean-Bernard Carillet As a Paris-based (and Metz-born) journalist and photographer, I was delighted to re-discover my own turf while researching *France Trips 1*. I couldn't resist the temptation of exploring Burgundy and Beaujolais, if only to sample some of the best wines in the world. I confess a penchant for the Meursault whites (in Burgundy) and the Fleurie reds (in Beaujolais).

Gregor Clark My first epic French road trip came on Bastille Day at age 20. Nearly broke and hitchhiking towards my next fruit-picking job, I landed a 400km lift from a lost tourist and proceeded to spend the night winding through the fireworks-lit streets of every little village in Haute-Provence. To this day, I love nothing better than aimlessly wandering France's back roads in search of hidden villages and unexpected treasures. I contribute regularly to Lonely Planet's European and South American guidebooks.

Read more about Gregor at: lonelyplanet.com/members/gregorclark

OUR WRITERS

Alexis Averb... ...e family holiday
four and now vis... ...een back many
browsing markets ... ...anet's bestselling
in the Loire or car... ...orner of
in Provence, she ... ...especially soft
French. A travel write... ...en not in France,
lived in Antarctica for a... ...beaches and
sailboat, and is also a ... ...l. I'm also a regular
alexisaverbuck.com. ... ...ewspapers and
...Traveller. Check out
...y.com.

Read more ab...
members/...

...elyplanet.com/

MORE WRITERS

Published by Lonely Planet Publications Pty Ltd
ABN 36 005 607 983
1st edition – June 2015
ISBN 978 1 74360 709 1
© Lonely Planet 2015   Photographs © as indicated 2015
10 9 8 7 6 5 4 3 2 1
Printed in China

Although the authors and Lonely Planet have taken all reasonable care in preparing this book, we make no warranty about the accuracy or completeness of its content and, to the maximum extent permitted, disclaim all liability arising from its use.